Three Years
in a Walmart Parking Lot

Sharon Waters

For Cricket, Magic, and Milo
and all the friends and family
who made this a wondrous journey

Three Years in a Walmart Parking Lot

by Sharon Waters

ISBN: 978-0-578-40538-4

https://www.facebook.com/sharon.waters.5205

First Edition, 2019

Published in USA

Three Years
in a Walmart Parking Lot

Contents

Starting...1

On the Road..13

Early Days..31

The South...67

Solar Panels..85

Summer in Salem...................................95

Making Another Plan...........................103

In Others' Homes..................................113

Salem as Home......................................137

The Third Trip South............................151

Decisions..163

Landing..175

Starting

The beast grumbled and shuddered. Then nothing. I shifted in the driving seat, released a breath, and listened to my heartbeat. I turned the key again and the diesel engine roared to life. I looked along the dashboard for the controls I would need for the drive back to Salem. It was an unusually cold day, even for November, and I wanted to get going. Reviewing the transfer paperwork and signing the forms had taken longer than I expected. Now all I could think of was to be on my way.

Against the misgivings of my family, I had sold my house and moved in with a friend. I could no longer afford the house, and getting an apartment that didn't allow dogs was out of the question. Buying an RV had been in the back of my mind for some time and now I had done it. After scouring ads from across the country, I drove a few hours away to examine RVs firsthand at dealers in western Massachusetts. It was the end of the summer so prices were lower, but inventory was low as well. Plus, I had little knowledge of mechanics and what the technical descriptions meant. I hadn't thought layout to be important, but then I fell in love with one that was a perfect layout for me and was determined to buy it. A few days later, I came back with the check and sealed the purchase. Without ever having driven an RV, I put my foot on the gas pedal and turned onto the highway.

The only thing that gave me confidence was the height of the cabin. The view overlooking traffic was reassuring. Given that my rig was twenty-seven feet long, I needed all the visibility I could get.

Terrified, I drove at the ridiculously modest speed of 40 mph all the way back to Salem. Most of my first year I traveled at the slowest speed allowed. I was more like a barge drifting amongst the frenetic movement of the more maneuverable, less ponderous cars. But I was perched in my cabin with my heightened view of the road and of life as I started a journey that would take me three years and thousands of miles and test my ability to survive on my own. I discovered daily challenges during those years, but gained the discipline to get up and get moving every morning. I found relief at completing another piece of the journey as I pulled in every afternoon and discovered a sense of achievement for a lone woman, sixty-nine years old.

After two hours of driving and feeling as if I had sweated off ten pounds, I arrived back in Salem. I carefully maneuvered my leviathan chariot through the narrow colonial streets. At last I pulled into the driveway of my good friend, Margaret, who had offered me a place to stay while she took a month-long trip. I could use her house as a refuge and staging area while I shifted my life from a house with fenced lot to an RV. Margaret's wide driveway could accommodate my RV off-street as I transitioned from one life to another. I turned off the ignition and the diesel engine went quiet.

I was fortunate to have time at Margaret's home. I had sold my house in one day instead of the six months I expected, so I made a hasty and arduous exit. The stuff of my life filled every nook and cranny of my 1730s colonial and the move had immediate ramifications. I had to downsize—drastically.

As I had migrated from home-to-home, starting married life, having children, shifting from job-to-job and interest-to-interest, I accumulated great quantities of the infamous "stuff." A survey of my accumulations would show the books I'd read, where I'd lived and vacationed, and my interests in multiple projects. I'd had a period of fascination with vintage clothing and collected so much of it that I converted dresses and shawls into wall hangings. To enter my room was to think you'd entered the Victorian age. Velvet draped everything and sparkling costume jewelry adorned it.

After my vintage clothing period passed, I replaced it with a random assortment of rocks, fossils, and African masks. I had several Buddhas from Nepal, a collection of chicken feathers, art déco lighting fixtures, a dollhouse that I had worked on for months, and more cooking apparatus than anyone needs. I had a surfeit of flower pots, water sports paraphernalia, leather-working tools, and a room full of computers and their associated devices. There were tchotchke frogs, stone gargoyles, and a myriad of architectural salvage pieces acquired on my frequent trips to the Hudson Valley. I had stained glass doors used as room dividers, and once I'd had a functioning koi pond in my living room.

I could go on, but fundamentally, I was an organized hoarder. Stuff was orderly, but too abundant. When an item became buried, I bought duplicates and triplicates. I knew deep down that my home had become a container of stuff as much as a living space, and like others who secretly realized they had a problem, I watched the hoarding shows. I identified with keeping things because I was sure I might need it, it had meant something once, I had paid a lot for it, or I just needed the security of having it there.

I suspect keeping things beyond necessity has its roots in anxiety. The Scandinavians are noted for their happiness and spare living. So are Buddhists monks. They understand that stuff impedes what you really need to be happy. Now anything that wasn't practical and useful had to go.

I was fortunate to have help and knew that I needed it. My friend, Ruby, taught me the essentials of sorting and clearing out. She didn't allow sorting through things as they were stuffed in boxes or closets. Instead, we took everything out and put it in three piles: save, give away, and throw away. I had watched enough hoarding shows to know this process was right, but I needed a friend to insist on it. I could immediately appreciate the value of space and what a relief it was. In five minutes, I could remove everything and have an empty closet. In half an hour, with Ruby's help, I had three piles and two thirds of the clutter was packed to go. I learned that taking more than an hour to clean out a closet risks never getting it done, and moving faster reduces the anguish of parting with material things.

My cellar overwhelmed me. Everything that couldn't be faced was down there, especially the detritus of my now ex-partner who had increasingly spent his time at his mother's place over the last year. Most of the basement piles were his and had been accumulating unchecked for the fifteen years we shared the house. They were in an area that, under threat, had been off-limits. I had been living on egg-shells, constantly nervous that I would say the wrong thing or stray into a place where I wasn't permitted. It had prevented me from feeling comfortable anywhere in a home that should have been my sanctuary.

I called a clean out guy and was blessed with a sympathetic and understanding fellow who could have been straight out of a hoarders show. Ashen and faint, I instructed Carlos to just get rid of everything. Instead, he convinced me to sit, give myself time to overcome my nervousness, then evaluate each group of items before they were carted away. For each bin or crate of contents, I sat with it, considered its value or connection to me, and then let it go. With this review process, I wasn't burdened with guilt and regret later. Carlos taught me a method for facing decisions and parting with stuff. I approved a box of my old family pictures to get dumped, but he said no, it should be cleaned of the mouse droppings and kept. He was right that later I'd cherish those pictures, and I'm eternally grateful for what he did for me that day.

I carried what remained of the great purge to Margaret's house. Now the task was to figure how to fit it into the RV—or not. So much had been done and now I'd have to make more sorting decisions all by myself. It took a month to decide what I would need in the RV and what to put into a tiny storage unit, such as a few prized lamps and rugs. Since I could be gone for years, what was worth keeping at the cost of a storage fee? What clothes would I need? I was heading south, so I had the delusion I'd just need beach sandals and the occasional sweater. Where I got stuck most often was with the decorative objects, the comfort items, those buffers against anxiety. Fortunately my daughter, Peg, valued my photography prints—the natural scenes and the surreal photo compositions that had taken me months to create—and moved them to her home. The pictures done by my artist friends I couldn't part with, so they went into storage. And I would be eminently thankful for saving my winter gear and clothing.

For the first few weeks, I got used to staying in Margaret's house. My life in the colonial and the houses before it was gone. But I had no house upkeep or bills to worry about that November, and I was still in my familiar neighborhood on the shore of Collins Cove. I walked the same routes with my dogs and had all the comforts of home. But with winter approaching, I'd have to be gone before snow buried the RV. Some days I took things to storage. Other days I turned on the heaters in the RV and started to create what would be my new home. The RV had a back bedroom that was slowly becoming my sanctuary, and just before the snows, I moved in.

While outfitting the RV, I considered my general health and what impact it could have on the RV trip. I had a backlog of pills to take with me but I'd have to refill prescriptions along the way. I hoped to eventually dispense with them, but that would take time and I didn't know if I could. I had an inhaler for a respiratory problem that had plagued me over the last year. I suspected it came from mold and mice droppings in the basement that Carlos had cleared out, and my breathing was easier although still chronically difficult.

I'd had constant anxiety resulting from the stress of my relationship, and worried about the long-term prognosis. I didn't want to depend on pills as a perpetual coping solution and wasn't keen on trading the relief that medications provided for their side effects—the doctors minimized them but I didn't.

I'd had surgery on my back in the spring before selling the house. With Ruby's nursing, I'd survived several days in bed and weeks of recovery. It was supposed to relieve painful pinched nerves in my lower back, but it wasn't the complete cure I'd hoped for. I was up and walking, but it was still painful and required modification in my days—no heavy lifting and I needed to avoid stairs. The single floor and lack of furniture to move around in the RV should help.

November became December. I had planned to leave by the first, but dental work delayed the start of the trip. For the first time in my life I needed a root canal, and I didn't want it to be a problem on the road. So I stayed for appointment after appointment until they finished with the drilling and the cap. But now I was facing the beginning of January, and it was turning unusually cold, even for Massachusetts. I heard rumors of something called the North Polar Vortex, which would influence the oncoming winter. After the first heavy snowstorm, I dug out the RV and started on my way. I'd be heading south, so logic assured me that an incrementally lower latitude would gradually be warmer each day. I had a lot to learn about the weather.

So why, many have asked, did I sell my house, relinquish my possessions, and leave behind a city I loved in the dead of winter? One might guess things had not been going well at home and indeed there was a physical threat and psychological angst that went on behind closed doors. It had reached the point of calling the police as my personal relationship of twenty years disintegrated. I'd had it with the coping mechanisms of the day, therapists and pills. I had good friends, but I needed the search for self that would distance me from both the close-to-home problems and the wider cultural expectations for a woman my age that were messing with my head.

Alone in the house after my partner left, I reorganized and the beginning of a lovely summer opened the door to more peaceful days. But my old and roughly built colonial house required never-ending repairs I couldn't afford. The house sold quickly in August and by fall I was hopscotching to Margaret's and then to the RV.

I faced raised eyebrows over my decisions. I was older, female, and by myself—this was not what I was expected to do. I was nudged toward aging gracefully in some assisted living arrangement or at least where everyone was safely over fifty-five. To me, that sounded like signing up for a living death, like treading water before drowning.

I was struck by a number of people—women in particular—who when they learned of my intended RV caper, said "I wish I could do that." What invisible thing tells people what they can and cannot do? What cultural conditioning and restraints become mental sand traps for one's possibilities and potential? It was a cultural message I was familiar with, but decided to ignore. All I would have to do is dismiss the dire warnings, become proficient in everything mechanical, and improve my knowledge of digital navigation. Many believe that aging is an inevitable path toward reduced ability to learn and evolve. I'd have to disprove that.

I pulled out of Margaret's driveway into a journey that would show me, as a habitually dependent person, what I was capable of on my own. To soften the impact, I drove no more than fifty to a hundred miles per day. I realized this was ridiculous, but I gave myself and my three pet companions time to adjust to the roaring engine and the overwhelming feeling of massive weight behind me. The rear camera was foggy, and it took me several days to properly align the side mirrors. I was terrified of passing other vehicles, and since I wasn't doing more than 50 mph, for most of my first trip south I clung to the slow lane and counted the miles until my next stop. I planned to see friends and stay with family, but because of my short driving periods I was mostly overnighting in Walmart parking lots. The rest was learning and processing time.

I had done my research. I knew that living in an RV was possible, even desirable, as a tiny house and that a few places encouraged free parking for RVs, Walmart in particular. RVs aren't welcome in many parking lots and, even a few Walmarts restrict them now due to trucks running diesel engines all night, loud teenagers holding parking lot parties and other troubles. But this was early in the 'stealth traveling' craze and the Walmart chain became my overnight stops up and down the eastern US.

Walmart had good reason to welcome RV travelers. Those affluent enough to buy an RV have money to spend and need the food and sundries that Walmart has to offer. This applied to me as well, and I purchased everything from unappetizing meals to miniature tea-pots and coffee makers that were workable in the limited space. Occasionally a Walmart stop rewarded me with a Wi-Fi connection. For my first trip, though, I especially needed free parking and a place that could offer warmth and safety if I needed it.

On the Road

My first stop was a visit with my brother-in-law, David, and his partner, Pam. They lived a few hours' drive from Salem, but I was still in Massachusetts and the comfort of the familiar. David had designed and built a gorgeous home beneath the shadow of Mount Greylock. My dogs, Cricket and Magic, had the trail up the mountain and a large lawn to run in. I had a lovely downstairs guest room artfully decorated by Pam, along with my own bathroom and a coffee maker in a quiet space of my own. I shared a delicious homemade dinner with my hosts, and Pam prepared a special meal for the dogs.

It was so pleasant there I could have stayed forever, but with my RV dominating the driveway and blocking the garbage guys, it was necessary to get out of the way. This was one of the most important lessons and I learned it over and over in my travels. RVs are welcome for a visit—but not for long. Unless you are paying for an assigned space, eventually you must move on, blend into crowded parking lots, or fade into remote places.

RVs are considered unsightly, a blemish on residential suburban neighborhoods. If you stay a day or two, you are a visitor. If you stay longer, you are trailer trash. I learned the rules of RV parking and noticed how they became more restrictive over the three years of my travels. Most towns have an ordinance regarding how long an RV can park on residential property, particularly if the RV is being lived in. They limit on-street parking to certain times of day and particular times of the year. Tourists who spend money in souvenir shops and restaurants are welcome—those seeking cheap living are not.

Parking is one of the first things anyone thinking of purchasing an RV should consider. Every RV owner gets asked, "What kind of RV would you recommend?" The answer is "That depends," because it depends on the lifestyle you have in mind. If you want to drive to a national park and stay there for two weeks, a small-to-moderately sized RV will do fine. If you plan on heading to Florida for the winter where you will hook up to utilities and stay put for five months, a larger model might be your pick. If you are a musician who travels from one urban gig to another but want to avoid expensive hotel bills, you'll want a van that doesn't suggest it's your residence so you can get away with urban street parking short term.

RVs have three major classes: A, B+, and C. A fifty foot Class A provides house-like luxuries and space, but you'll be limited to campgrounds that allow this size. If you like to get around, you'll be handicapped by the size of your Class A and where it's acceptable. Some ferries allow RVs, but none will carry one over thirty-three feet. A Class C is smaller, boxy, made in modular pieces and is less expensive. A Class B+ (and no one *really* knows why it's called B+), is more custom built, less boxy, van-like, and more expensive than a comparable Class C. Vans and RV truck toppers can be the least expensive home away from home. Although they offer fewer amenities and less space, they are the most flexible for parking and the easiest on your fuel bill.

My RV was unusual in its length of twenty-seven feet. Far more are either twenty-five feet or thirty-three. The twenty-five foot varieties have a drawback, IMHO. They are a bit short for an extra room and the manufacturers don't know what to do with the few feet of left-over space. So they break up the bathroom into a sink and shower on one side of the aisle, the toilet on the other. How awkward is that? Thirty-three feet will get you a separate back room, but you're a bit large for easy parking.

My brilliant twenty-seven footer was exactly two car lengths long, perfect for double length, nose-to-nose parking spaces in parking lots and anywhere I could find two spaces together on the street. The best part of my RV design was in its width. Almost all RVs are eight-and-a-half feet in width. Mine was a narrow seven-and-a-half—just that of a car. I managed street parking often and easily and it was a small price to pay for a slightly narrow interior. I had a diesel Gulf Stream Mini Cruiser, which had one of the best designs ever made for someone like me. I never regretted my choice for the kind of traveling I did. I easily parked Twenty-Seven, as I named her, on the circle outside my brother-in-law's house and in driveways of friends and family.

From that first night at David's, I learned the critical job of checking weather, road conditions, and my planned overnight for the following day. As I came to know oh so well, the weather had a distinct influence on where, how, and when I traveled. The predicted polar vortex arrived that night, bringing with it snow and plunging temperatures. I decided to make my departure the next day and head for warmer climates.

In the morning I packed up my few belongings from the guest room, said goodbye to my hosts, put the dogs in the RV, and crawled down the slippery, snowy, icy, terrifying incline from the house to the main road. It was freezing and windy, but my first planned Walmart stop was only seventy miles away. I'd have the afternoon to contemplate my venture, find Wi-Fi to check the weather, and walk the dogs around the parking lot. My reasoning at the time was that I would be incrementally farther south, so it would be incrementally warmer. Even one degree would give me hope of eventually getting above zero. I had much to learn about weather patterns of the eastern US. This 'incrementally warmer by latitude' belief is not true. During a polar vortex visit you can freeze your butt off all the way to Georgia. And it just kept getting colder, every day.

Frigid air from the Arctic and Canada can slither down the humped back of the Appalachians all the way to the Everglades. One is beyond the reach of bone-chilling cold only if you are below the mainland, far down on the finger of Florida that reaches into the Gulf. Even then, there are days when Florida manatees huddle in water heated by power plants or shiver in the chilly coastal waters. I took to checking the national weather map on Intellicast several times a day. When the weather gods hurled Arctic bolts southward, inland Atlanta could be colder than seaside Boston, and often during that winter it was.

You can survive in an RV in the winter, but few are made for it. Unless you have purchased an RV specifically built and insulated for chilly weather, the assumption is that you are at the beach or campground and it's eighty degrees—most RVs have air conditioning. What you can work with in cold weather, even without insulation, is the smaller space. The first thing I did was cover the bedroom window with blankets, and eventually I recruited an ancient sleeping bag for my bedroom insulation. The old sleeping bag was a pre-lightweight synthetic model and had thick cotton stuffing. Heavy and stiff, it could be molded into the window frame. I separated the driving cabin from the interior by hanging heavy blankets and at night I closed the bedroom sliding door so Cricket and Magic, my cat Milo, and I were huddled in a space just large enough for a mattress.

In an igloo-sized space protected from the wind, you can manage. Your most essential item is a sleeping bag if you are going to be in cold weather —mountain climbers and explorers know this. Stay dry, out of the wind, climb into your sleeping bag, and you will likely see another day. Add two small dogs and a cat and you will be comfortably warm.

I headed south and in the early afternoon I pulled into the first Walmart of the journey. I had overcome the terror of starting out, had avoided traffic incidents, and was safely parked at my day's destination. I was elated to have made that first leg—all I had to do was repeat it a thousand times. I liked the sense of isolation and invisibility, hiding in plain sight, removed from anything threatening. There were no stern looks of disapproval, no mail with bad news or phone calls I didn't want to take. I was inconspicuous, unseen, untraceable. I had my cell phone but rarely answered it. A rented mailbox in Salem served as my address, but I was nowhere, drifting in a sea of parking lots, highways, and traffic.

On arrival, I checked that everything in the RV was in order for the rest of the day. I released the few items I had lashed or tucked in safe places, picked up anything that had been hurled from its place as we rocked down the highway, and covered the windows for privacy. I was cocooned, safe, and anonymous in the crush of shopping mall humanity. My first venture out the door was to take Cricket and Magic for a walk and to check for Wi-Fi bars. After several days of Walmart stops, I discovered Redbox DVD rentals just inside the Walmart doors. The dogs were allowed inside those doors, and soon they expected that choosing DVDs was part of their walking routine. For a few minutes we were warm and out of the wind and then back in the RV we decompressed from travel in the afternoons.

At every stop, there were the usual chores to do.

If I wasn't close enough to pick up Walmart Wi-Fi, I'd restart the RV and move closer to the building. If the Walmart didn't have guest Wi-Fi, I found another store in the parking lot that did. Arriving earlier in the day increased the odds that I'd make a connection instead of getting stuck in the outskirts of the parking lot. After I settled, I'd run the generator, power up the computer, and go straight to MapQuest. Somewhere farther south between fifty and eighty miles away there would be another twenty-four hour Walmart Superstore. I didn't live at any one Walmart—I lived at all of them, one after another.

I rarely parked at any particular one for more than a day. But in those afternoons and evenings, I had time to think, regroup, and settle my mind. After I had shopped for a few items, checked out Redbox with the dogs, and made notes for the next day's travel, my mind was free.

I always made sure to write everything down on paper in case I couldn't get Wi-Fi or the computer wouldn't start. In a home, you expect appliances to be dependable and it's an unanticipated disruption if they aren't. My days were the opposite. I was ecstatic when things worked, always prepared if they didn't. Over the years I filled up several notebooks of daily stops, the addresses, whether they had Wi-Fi, and the best places to park.

One device, though, just *had* to work. My GPS was critical, and I couldn't have managed a single day in the three-year trip without it. I am hopelessly directionally challenged, and I was on unfamiliar roads all the time. Louise, a friend who had just begun her RV living, suggested GPS devices made for RVers. They have a place for entering the weight and dimensions of your RV, and it's supposed to alert the driver to hazards specific to their dimensions, such as a low bridge. Its warnings didn't always work, but it had a large screen that showed good pictures of the road ahead. The GPS lady voice spoke calmly and reliably at two miles, a half mile, and when I arrived at the destination. She warned me ahead about turnoffs, and whether I should be in the right lane or the left. Without that voice guiding me this would be a very different story.

Early in my trip, I stopped at a few RV stores that had racks of paraphernalia and the latest maps and books. I purchased a couple maps, but over my three years of travel, I never opened a physical map or guidebook. I finally threw them out. I couldn't consult a hard copy map while driving the RV—I never took my eyes off the road. There was no way I could have navigated the complexity of ramps and exits on the Atlanta and DC beltways or found my way back from a wrong turn without the GPS lady's voice talking me through it. I always knew how many miles I had to go and what time I'd arrive. I was totally, thoroughly, dependent on GPS devices and eventually had three of them. When one failed or couldn't find a location, I'd swap in another.

I came to love and appreciate digital maps. Printed maps can never match their ability to zoom in or out, to change detail and perspective. I could find pet shops near my destination Walmart in advance, have a satellite view of the shopping complex, or see the geological perspective of the terrain. I could locate the closest propane station, calculate its distance from Walmart, and plan the best route to get there the next morning. I was, and still am, completely in love with that technology.

But once I had done my research for the following day, it was downtime, dinner, and evening study or entertainment. If the Wi-Fi signal was strong enough, I'd watch Netflix. If not, I'd walk over to Redbox or the DVD discount bin in Walmart. Over time, I accumulated a collection of $2.50 - $5.00 DVDs that filled several cloth tote bags. Walmart grocery shopping was banal but cheap and adequate for essentials. Sharing a snack with the dogs and Milo became a daily ritual during evening movie or reading time.

I picked up books, especially in the South, and read many about the Civil War while my back-roads wandering took me through historical places of battle. I stopped at just about every city, town, brook and farm that Sherman passed through on his march to the sea while the books and documentaries recounted their stories. At a Civil War reenactment, I got to see the H. L. Hunley submarine and read the chronicle of the brave crews who perished in her. While there, I heard the astonishing story of how reenactors in period dress showed up from across the US to honor their sacrifice during a commemorative event.

Cricket, Magic, and Milo were my best friends, my solace, and protection. I was traveling alone, a single woman of a certain age. But I had pledged my life to my pets, and them to me. The dogs especially earned their badge as my guardians. A woman's best friends aren't diamonds—they're her dogs and her cat.

The animals were lively, bright, and funny—I think uniquely entertaining for their kind. Milo was less standoffish than most cats, and Cricket and Magic, as Schipperkes, demanded attention constantly. Schipperkes are said to be as intelligent as a seven-year-old child and are known for inventing games with their owners. If I didn't think of something for them to do, they would create fun for all of us.

I owed them for their devotion, for which they are also renowned. I thought back on the time when I was swimming at our summer cottage lake with my daughter, Peg, and her kids. We were quite a way out, and I was diving to clear lake weeds from our swimming area. Poor Magic, terribly concerned, whimpered on the shore. Finally he plunged into the water and swam out, making desperate attempts to save me from what he was sure was drowning. My dogs are only fourteen pounds but would take on anyone or anything to assure my safety. I owed my fur friends the best care and companionship I could give them. We were kindred fellows on an adventure.

That first night was a triumph. We had made it through the day and found our resting place for the night. We were chilly, but surviving. Most systems worked although the hot water for the shower was not cooperating. I had food, shelter, and the pets for company. I could disconnect from the past and focus on this journey down the highway.

For a time I survived well enough on a Social Security paycheck. I had dismissed the apartments and senior housing arrangements that disallowed dogs. I wanted to expand, not constrict, my experiences and insights and in spite of the naysayers, I was convinced I could in the RV. The only thing standing in my way was the weather.

The polar vortex arched across the country and descended on the East, freezing everything rock solid. It went from single digits to below zero. Winds howled. Snow accumulated. Increasing my miles south didn't have the warming effect I'd anticipated. Instead, I drove into the icy face of winter, which was to challenge me to my marrow.

While the generator worked, my days were manageable, survivable. But I had a lot to learn about generators and the efficiency of RV systems. My generator ran on propane, but unlike a house heating system, it's located on the exterior. In exceptionally cold weather it's heating all outdoors until the heated air is blown inside. Later research informed me that the blower uses the most energy, so between the outside placement and the blowers, it's a serious fuel waster. After a few sobering calamities, I learned the thermostat connects to a mysterious "brainboard" hidden in the RV walls. The brainboard measures power available for the thermostat, which was periodically failing to signal that it was cold and time for another blast of heat.

It puzzled me why after being comfortably warm for a few hours, the thermostat would fail. At night as the temperature slipped below zero, the RV would grow cold and besides being chilled myself, I worried about my fur kids. Like a soldier called to duty, I'd get up and head for the one thing I could rely on—the diesel engine. RV dogma insists diesel engines often don't start in cold weather, but I was fortunate and the engine was my lifesaver. Twenty minutes of running the engine revived the generator, which resurrected the thermostat to trigger the heat. Wake up freezing, run the engine to get the generator going, then wait for the revived thermostat to send warmth—I repeated this half hour routine every two hours of the night for the next three months.

I never did locate the brainboard. I'm not sure if it's a myth or just a way to assign blame when the system fails, but I'd heard the brainboard explanation from one of the few people who serviced my RV that could make things work. What I suspected was the battery, especially as I explored the relationship of engines, electrical systems, and power. I could get heat, but only at the cost of sleep and sanity. Besides having to restart the process every few hours, I was constantly out of propane. RVs don't need frequent propane refills in warm weather, but if you are hunkering down in one spot for the winter you need a sizable propane tank. Since I was on the move, I had to find a new propane source every other day as the polar vortex pursued me down I-95.

I soon learned that there are two types of nozzle fittings for dispensing propane and frequently the place you stop at will have only one—but not the one you need to fill your built-in RV tank. Often the fittings would be for canisters, the propane guy wouldn't be in until Tuesday, or it was the weekend or a holiday. My nightly ritual, besides locating the next Walmart, was to find a propane station nearby and to call ahead to learn my chances for a refill. I was obsessed with having enough propane, overjoyed when I had a full tank, and nervous when it was less than half full. If I didn't have enough for a full night, I was on the hunt for it.

Early Days

It took a lot out of my day to keep all the systems going—checking on them, learning the particulars of my electrical, water, and heat components, and keeping tanks topped up with fuel. In the morning I secured movable objects with bungee cords, reviewed my itinerary, checked fuel levels, and then hit the highway. Diesel and/or propane had to be acquired before I'd be assured enough to settle for the night, and I wanted to be parked and settled well before dark. It wasn't a lot of daily driving, but it was a crash course in RV living and maintenance.

I enjoyed starting the day with hot coffee, and Cricket and Magic liked getting out the door in a new place. They delighted in meeting people and finding fresh dog smells to sniff. If I was close enough to Wi-Fi, I checked the weather and the morning news. Then I could complete the chores if I concentrated on the relief of having them done. Securing all objects was a pain, but I would soon be on the road. I'd tick off the miles and stop at propane or diesel services I'd noted the night before. If I managed a fill-up without sideswiping a concrete post in the gas station, I was doing well. Pulling in and parking for the night was a highlight, a relief—a psychological pat on the back for having made it.

I learned the rules of the road for an RV. After leaving Massachusetts, I turned onto the picturesque Taconic Parkway in New York that I had driven so many times before. Fifteen miles later I was escorted off by a State Trooper who informed me I had missed a sign (had I?) that said no RVs. Bridges on the Taconic are low, stone curbs make turning off impossible, and my $250 RV GPS had neglected to inform me of the prohibition or the danger. Lesson learned. The trooper escorted me to the next exit where I'd have to find a new route to my next Walmart destination in Danbury, Connecticut.

I never figured out why Danbury has particularly friendly shopping mall people. They loved the dogs, and more than any other place over the next three years, I was stopped to explain and show off my wondrous Schipperke canines. Dogs are excellent ice-breakers and a good judge of character. I was more at ease and trusting with people who were sincerely interested in my pups and they would tell me their own dog stories. One fellow lingered over Cricket and Magic for several minutes, and then shared that his dog had died the previous week. It was his last connection to his departed wife since they had picked out the dog together thirteen years ago. There was quiet, a few tears, and a hug with a stranger.

Another fellow just flipped over the dogs. "They're Schipperkes! Can I see them, pat them?" Then came the story of his beloved Schipperke that had passed. I get that people are devoted to their Schipperkes as I am with mine. He'd leave us, then a few minutes later show up again for "just one more minute with the Schips." He seemed unable to pull himself away, so I invited him into the RV to spend time with the dogs. We had a lively, friendly conversation trading dog anecdotes, and I have stayed in touch with Lou ever since. In subsequent years I stopped by when I was in Danbury and parked at his house. We shared dinner, and he showed me the Schipperke costume he had worn for Halloween. Dogs are good at creating bonds, and Schipperkes are the best ambassadors.

As I crept slowly south and west, I had to find a way around New York City and Philadelphia. I was doing okay, but I wasn't ready to brave beltway travel. My GPS—besides forgetting about low bridges—disagreed with me about the best route. It was mistaken that I traveled at the speed limit and insisted I'd prefer high-speed routes over fewer miles. For someone who barely hit fifty, it was more realistic for me to take shorter routes at a lower speed. For the start, anyway. To sidestep suggested GPS routes, I'd input a series of shorter trips with destinations that circumnavigated the major urban centers. All I needed each day was a Walmart Superstore destination and the least challenging way to get there.

It was slow going, by choice and by necessity. And it was bitter cold and getting colder. I hung blankets over the windows and blocked off the driving cabin at night. I wore multiple layers and kept the dogs in their winter dog coats night and day. Milo was part Angora and the least affected, but he huddled up with me and the dogs in our sleeping bag at night. By the time we reached Middletown, NY, I was taking the dogs into Walmart to warm them up. The greeters didn't blink when I lined the bottom of a cart and placed both dogs inside. If I kept them in a cart and looked as if I did this all the time, I didn't get stopped. Having passed the test of entry, I headed for the back part of the store and wandered through mostly vacant aisles. While we soaked in warmth, I gave the dogs a whispered narration of candle collections, the colors and patterns of linens, and the wonders to be had in the dog food aisle. Then we went back across the windswept parking lot that could have been a remote tundra in Siberia.

The RV was livable as long as the dogs and I had enough layers for warmth during the day and bundled in the sleeping bag at night. We resolutely progressed through Allentown, Pennsylvania, then Lancaster, but the plunging temperatures of the 2014 North Polar Vortex were daunting. (From Wikipedia: "Temperatures fell to unprecedented levels, and low temperature records were broken across the United States.) The hot water wasn't working, although with the chill in the RV it wouldn't have been comfortable anyway. I envisioned a future archeologist digging me out like a frigid relic, frozen in an ice block. So I had no shower, only hot water from the stove for coffee. Changing clothes was brutal, so I kept it to a minimum. I was in civilization, but living as if I were in an ice age cave of ten thousand years ago.

York, PA, tested my resolve. We pulled in as usual in the early afternoon. There was time to plan the following day, relax, study, and cook a light supper before the animals and I crawled into bed. We had been on the road for several days, and I was coping, but tired. Buried as we were in blankets of warmth, I didn't wake that night to run the engine and generator to restart the thermostat. At dawn, I finally stirred and saw my breath freeze in the sliver of light piercing through a crack in the window barricade. It had dropped to twenty degrees in the RV and the water in the dogs' dish had frozen solid. The burner on the stove seemed like the only heat in the universe, and I drank a quick cup of coffee before preparing to head for the nearest propane station.

Extreme cold will defeat electronics. The engine started (thank the Goddess) and I held the GPS in front of a heat vent. Twenty minutes later it came to life, and I dashed out of the parking lot to find the nearest propane. The highway was almost deserted and I imagined a great many people were in their driveways sitting in frigid cars that refused to start. The wind picked up, blowing snow sideways across the roads. I felt colder than I had ever been in my life. Cricket made a sad noise and then fell unusually quiet. I looked over and both dogs were shivering. They looked back at me with bewilderment and anguish. They were worried and uncertain as to why something had gone so terribly wrong.

After driving a few miles I spotted an abandoned school lot that would be a safe place to park. I pulled over, cranked the cabin heat as high as it went with the engine running, tucked both dogs under my coat, and held them until they stopped shivering. Only Milo was unaffected and he just nestled further into the box of winter hats in the bunk.

After half an hour we were a few degrees warmer, so I started out for the propane station again. When we arrived, their filling nozzle was the wrong kind, so with sketchy directions from the people at that service stop I headed for another station. I had no specific address for the GPS, so it wasn't useful, and you don't just pull over to ask directions in an RV. After wandering around the outskirts of York I found the station, the nozzle fit, and I got propane.

By then it was afternoon and I was completely frazzled, so I set the GPS for the same Walmart I had left that morning. At least it would be something familiar after a desperate day. The raw cold had driven most people indoors, and the lot was nearly empty. I got out the leashes and took the dogs for a walk around the edges of the lot to do their business. I felt sorry for them, but it's the dogs' bargain with humans that they will poop and pee outside. The winds hounded us across the darkening lot, its frigid fingers blowing through gaps in my clothing and biting anything exposed with icy teeth.

Back in the RV, the systems were running again, and it was livable. I put together early dinner for myself, the dogs, and Milo, who remained unfazed by the day's events. The Wi-Fi worked, and I found a movie to stream. We all got in the sleeping bag and went no further that day. We had made no progress south, but we were alive and relieved to be safe and warm. Later I snapped a picture of my orchid plants that I had brought along for their floral cheer and posted it on

Facebook. They were just coming into bloom, but no one would know those buds never opened—they had frozen the previous night.

About 9:00 p.m., coldness invaded the RV once again. The generator wouldn't respond and the routine of cranking up the engine every two hours began. Yesterday came back to me—waking up to ice in the dogs' water bowl and the unnerving image of dogs shivering and sad. I bundled up, faced into the wind howling across the parking lot, and marched into Walmart. I bought seventeen candles in glass jars, carried them back to the RV, and lit every one of them. They covered every inch of counter space where I thought they wouldn't start a fire. With this primitive heating system set up like a dispersed fireplace, we wouldn't be cold again that night.

I had chosen a few books to take on the trip, and among those was one about the mindset of individuals facing life or death situations. I had read *The Perfect Storm*, which related the demise of a fishing boat and what its crew members must have felt as they drowned. The 'disaster' book I was reading in York described the mental state of those who are measuring their lives in minutes and how their thoughts are fixed on their imminent predicament and nothing else. I could identify with the narrowing of focus and the overwhelming relief of a survivor finding a floatable object after a shipwreck. With something to hang on to, you might survive for a few more hours, avoid the sharks, and eventually see a rescue plane on the horizon. That's how it felt to have solved the heat problem for at least one more passage of the dark hours. Tomorrow and everything else in the world didn't matter.

When I found stops that had Wi-Fi, I checked the RVers' online groups to see how others were doing. The messages were usually filled with reports of meet-ups with friends, suggestions of places to visit, and the standard problems that happen to RVs during travel. For the first time, I heard reports of those who had given up and were going home. The polar vortex was pushing far into the south, and there was sustained sub-zero weather in unaccustomed places. The Arctic cold had caught everyone off guard and was driving the less determined off the roads. But I kept going as there was nowhere else to go.

During the next few days I crept along the

highway and finally arrived in Frederick, Maryland. It was just a short distance to where my friends, Kathy and Al, lived in Boyds, but I planned to stop here to get myself presentable. I had been on the road, freezing, for over a week and had not showered. I tried to get the water heater going one more time, gave up, and suffered through a hurried shower with water just above freezing. It was shockingly, painfully cold, and did little good. The next day I arrived at my friends' house looking no doubt like a disheveled, half-frozen bird that had crash-landed on their porch.

The walls of Kathy's house are a soft, warm peach color. Magnificent paintings and lithographs of aging ships accentuate the walls and large windows frame a valley with horses grazing on rolling pastures. Time is unhurried and every evening a crackling fire warmed the living room where cheese, crackers, and drinks were graciously laid out. I had my own room, and when the others had something else to do, the dogs and I curled up on the bed with a book in comfort and security. Milo held his own in the RV, and for a few days we were clean, well fed, and anxiety-free. The last night we watched *Life of Pi* together and escaped into that mystical tale.

After a few days of visiting, the weather mellowed so it was time to make the best of it and head south again. I checked things in the RV—diesel (how much, when would I have to find a gas station?), generator working? lights? everything tied down? the next destination programmed into the GPS?—and then we were off. RV traveling requires discipline first thing every day of new travel—not to check means trouble later in the day. Dealing with all systems first became a thoroughly ingrained habit. I'm not in the RV any more, but that discipline sticks with me. Anything I'm not looking forward to gets done first—I just do it, with my mind on the completion, not the drudgery of the task.

Besides daily discipline, I reached beyond my comfort level. I had to manage failures and get places by myself. Before taking off on my venture, I had followed several RVer lists and bulletin boards. Most women were married and in traditional roles. Men did the maintenance and navigation while women did sandwiches. In these circumstances, if a husband died, the wife was helpless to continue. I was chief cook, driver, maintenance man, and navigator by default. I became knowledgeable and proficient in ways I never would have if it hadn't been essential. It was learning by immersion, and learn I did.

This venture arrived late in my life. In my youth, my father would have disapproved while my mother wept, but they were gone. In adulthood, I had young children to care for, then post-marriage, I would have been belittled by my long-term companion. My kids didn't approve of my escapade and were immersed in their own lives. But the only ones dependent on me now were the dogs and Milo, and they were fine with this undertaking.

I had pulled out the packed away pictures, the ones Carlos had me save, of those hardy women in my family who were my role models. My paternal grandmother became a physician in 1900. One of my exceptional aunts accomplished something new every year of her life—such as teaching yoga to the other vagabond travelers on cargo ships to foreign lands, attaining her real estate license, or writing a book of poetry—until she died at ninety-six. My maternal grandmother lived in an uninsulated cabin, got water by breaking pond ice with an ax, and slept next to the only heat source, the fireplace, all winter. Their achievements and strengths were mostly ignored in the family, but they were speaking to me from wherever their spirits were.

My primary motivation, though, was the dogs. Since I left my troubled relationship and couldn't support a house on my own, I had to find another place, another way. But where to go? Few apartments allow dogs and I refused to part with them or Milo. I'd live on the street, in my car, or take a job as a lighthouse keeper, but Cricket, Magic, and Milo had to stay with me. They got along fine with each other and habitually slept with me, wherever we were. Keeping the pets was a major determinant that plunged me into the three-year long river of highways and parking lots.

Schipperkes are better known as Belgian barge dogs. They are a 500-year-old breed no longer directly related to any other. Schipperke ancestors were a large herding dog in Belgium that got shrunk in size but not relative dimensions. Their long, wolf-like snouts with rows of rat-catching teeth distinguish them from their miniaturized cousins with short faces. Most often black with a noticeable neck ruff, they are distinctive and striking. Dogs of this breed are particularly smart, inquisitive, and alert and serve their humans in many ways. They are herders, excellent ratters, and the best of guard dogs. Their small size averaging fifteen pounds limits damage they might do to intruders, but they are suspicious creatures that warn by barking at anything or anyone they decide is a danger. They are strikingly bold, and I have seen mine chase after an astonished bear.

Schipperke owners become besotted with them and often call them "nurse dogs" or "heart dogs." If an owner is sick, these lively companions trade officious guarding duties for huddling close to an ailing human, keeping vigil for as long as it takes. Both Magic and Cricket showed this trait. They insisted on being entertained and busy—unless I was bedridden with my back problems. Then they huddled right by my side until I was on my feet. When they were feeling lively, I hoped the two dogs would amuse and distract each other, but they regarded me as "one of them" and insisted I join in their games. That meant Cricket wanted to roughhouse with me her way while Magic preferred joyous games of fetch. Instead of playing together, the two dogs meant I was twice as busy entertaining them. Remarkable for focused staring at their owners, Schipperkes are acutely aware of their caretaker's movements and moods. It's said that while other dogs may look at you, Schipperkes look right into your being, as I felt Cricket and Magic did with me. They are my best friends, soul mates, and the boldest of protectors. Like others of their Schipperke breed, Cricket and Magic have a unique ability to banish the shadows and cobwebs in human psyches.

Many Schipperkes live their whole lives on boats, so their transition to the RV and travel was natural. My guess was that Milo would be unhappy, but to my surprise, he was happier than ever. The over-cabin bunk became Milo's hangout where he'd pass contented hours nestled in a basket of hats. To my amazement, he never showed a blink of disturbance at the loud and rumbling diesel engine and generator noises. Instead, he delighted in having me and the dogs for constant company. At night he'd join us in the back bedroom, curl up next to the dogs and purr into the night.

The idea of separating people from their pets as superfluous, nonessential elements to our lives disturbs me. During one summer of our trip, Milo went missing for almost two months. I was distraught beyond heart-broken and eventually wrote a small book about his loss and recovery, *Milo*. I revealed how worry over Milo's fate pervaded my days and blocked engagement with friends and family until I got him back. The people who feel the importance of pets understood it, others, not so much. For me, the journey wouldn't have happened without them.

I still reasoned that latitude mattered, that the North Polar Vortex would respect those imaginary parallels. I had rounded the northern cities and had covered 500 miles south and west. I was leaving Maryland and for the first time in my life was driving in territory below the Mason Dixon Line. I believed it should be a slightly warmer, but that winter it was not. It was zero during the day and subzero with fearsome winds at night.

The pets adjusted to the confinement due to the cold. Milo seemed happier with our situation since we were constantly together. Cricket and Magic would have liked to be out more, but they seemed to understand the temperature problem and accepted the RV as home. Their behavior even improved in some ways. Where they'd had occasional lapses in judgement about where peeing was acceptable at home, they never made that mistake in the RV. They made a natural adjustment as if they were living in a den.

Except for stops with friends and family, every night we parked at Walmart. I began to consider alternatives. North of the Carolinas, RV camp-sites generally close the last day of October so they weren't an option. Truck stops welcome RVs and they have their advantages—fuel is always available, many have showers with towels for five to ten dollars, and there is Wi-Fi. The flip side is the constant running of diesel engines, noise and toxic fumes. So I stayed with Walmart as a place to shop for food, to have a quiet night, and as a source of movie DVDs.

When I had my home, I owned a Mac Pro linked to double screens for graphics and web design, which had been my job, and I did photo editing as well. It was perfect in the computer room of my house, but the desktop computer with all its peripherals was too bulky for the RV. The luxury of space gone, I traded the Mac Pro to a friend for computer conversion services and bought an iMac. Anything smaller wouldn't have served my needs, and notebooks and laptops aren't as hardy. Why a Mac instead of a PC? As everyone knows, it's a love thing with Mac people.

What I later came to understand and appreciate was the capacity for radio reception—the ability to pick up Wi-Fi at a distance—was double for the iMac over any laptop. It was too big to cart into a coffee shop, but I didn't want to spend hours in a coffee shop anyway. Instead, I had the increased capacity to receive Wi-Fi signals while parked outside a reasonably strong source. Then I could photo edit, write, check emails, stream documentaries, surf the web, or watch movies far into the night. I didn't want to leave the RV, and I was fortunate in that I rarely had to.

I'd use my phone and walk around a shopping mall with the dogs to locate a signal—those "bars." I'd park as close as possible, keeping in mind which end of the RV was nearest the source since even a few feet could make a difference. I'd check signal strength throughout the twenty-seven foot RV as well. At one stop I could only get a signal if I moved my computer to the top bunk above the driving cabin. I hauled up the computer and the dogs and Milo joined us. I put up a portable gate to keep us, packed as we were, from tumbling off our upper ledge. We spent the night up there—anything to get Wi-Fi and connect to the outside world.

Besides parting with a big computer, I divorced from Microsoft. Before I left, I bought the whole suite—MS Office with Word, Excel, and PowerPoint. But Microsoft didn't like the installation and screamed foul messages at me every time I tried to load it each day. I called and complained, and spent months typing in a thirty-two digit registration number. After two thousand entries of that exhaustingly long number, Microsoft informed me I had reached my limit, and I was cut off completely.

I longed for the days when you bought an application on disk and you owned it instead of downloading it. But the major applications companies want you to download, not buy disks, and to have a Wi-Fi connection to prove your identity, your ownership rights, or whether you paid your latest rental fee before getting access. I understand the piracy concern, but it was hindering me. Like other bad baggage, I left the use of everything Microsoft.

Back on the road, I learned and took some RV rules to heart. Safety is paramount, and if I had to break the rules because of RV size, then I did. I encountered the need for exceptions when my GPS inadvertently led me through a congested city center on one of my earliest excursions. There's no going through red lights or making illegal turns, but if I had to maneuver out of the way, I made decisions for the best outcome regardless of the rules. Once I had to pass under an old stone bridge bearing a sign assuring drivers that anything less than eleven feet could pass underneath. My RV was ten feet, eight inches high. It took me fifteen minutes to progress under that bridge since I got out every few inches forward to check my clearance. I ignored the irritated drivers behind me, and they were just lucky I didn't get stuck or they'd never have arrived home that day.

I learned the systems of the RV and became more comfortable with the driving—the elevation of the driver's seat and rear-view camera were helpful with the adjustment. But I would have to make improvements in power for the house systems. I had an electric microwave and a gas range with three burners. They worked well for the whole trip and made decent cooking possible. The heat and electric systems, though, needed a serious upgrade to be efficient and affordable. Starting everything up every two hours and the never-ending need for propane was expensive and exhausting. With access to Wi-Fi, I spent more and more time researching solar power for RVs.

This alerted me to the problem of lacking a fixed address. The first question in any service phone call is invariably, "Where are you located?" Everything involving an installation depends on where you are, so solar panel information was listed by state and it applied to residential homes. The home solar panel installers gave me little guidance, so I visited RV stores for my next foray into the possibilities.

At the big RV chains, the front door receptionist indicates the direction of the service desk. At the service area you meet the guy who gets the scheduler. There is the under manager, the head manager, and behind them the main mechanic in the back service bay. And behind him is a quiet little fellow who will be doing your work.

I don't want to disparage the RV retail chains, but I discovered their mechanics can have little skill beyond cars. RVs aren't cars, and cars they have worked on don't have solar panels. Plus, an RV houses multiple systems from microwaves to refrigerators and the power complications that accompany each of those systems. After going through the lineup of greeters, schedulers, managers, and a tier of mechanics, I was quoted a price of $1,600 total for solar panels and labor. As a novice, it took hours of online RV blog reading time and serious thinking before I realized that this was for installing the solar panels, but they might not be hooked up to anything. No one mentioned power storage, batteries, or inverters. I'd read stories of astonished RV newbies who landed in this situation. I went back to my research drawing board.

RVers need the connection and advice from other RVers, and it's not hard to find online groups. Reviewing a long list of personal horror stories can make the newbie such as myself cautious before signing commitments that involve a lot of money and affect my quality of living. I began to bypass the major RV stores except to spend the night in their parking lot after buying a few supplies I didn't really need. An increasing amount of my time was spent online researching solar panels for RVs. I learned two essential pieces of knowledge: 1. Solar panel success depends on the system as a whole, not just the solar panels. 2. If you don't make the effort to understand and have it done right the first time, you could be paying for it again—or you are just darn out of luck.

I had money enough for one pass at solar panels, and if I failed, my RV living would be gravely compromised. My secondhand RV was equipped with only one lead-acid battery suited for quick discharge. It was appropriate for starting a car but stored little and discharged quickly—so quickly that in a couple hours I was out of stored energy. When I embarked on my trip, I had no notion of my battery handicap, but I was learning in the solar panel discussions.

Upon my arrival in Burlington, North Carolina, my battery analysis began in earnest. All was fine that morning when I got propane, but suddenly the generator wouldn't start, and it promised to be yet another night below zero. I discovered the generator problem on Friday afternoon and was desperate to find a repair shop before the weekend. My panicky logic reasoned that if something wasn't starting, I should visit the nearby repair shop specializing in starters for automotive systems. I got a new battery there, which didn't help, but had my first experience with real southern politeness and hospitality, which did.

The starter service guys were sorry the new battery didn't help, then consulted among themselves for the best RV guy and looked up his phone number and location for me. That was so much better than "sorry, can't help you." It was getting late, the sun was setting, and the temperature plummeted. I called the RV repair fellow they suggested who was fifty miles away. He was exceptionally gracious as well, and promised to service my ailing RV the next morning.

Spending the night in the RV without heat would not do for the animals, so I pulled into an inexpensive—okay, very cheap—looking motel. I crossed the blustery parking lot carrying Cricket, next Magic, and finally Milo. I brought in any orchids that had survived the freezing, enough food to call dinner, and a few sundries that would get me through the night. I contemplated a hot shower and included a bottle of frozen hair dye in the necessities I brought over. The dogs enjoyed the spacious room while Milo paced and howled. He was so contented with his RV life that he protested noisily at being removed.

While the dogs settled and Milo complained, I changed out of my ice-coated clothes and defrosted the bottle of hair dye. I wondered before starting out if I should keep dying my hair the unusual colors that were acceptable in Salem, and even though it might be a social risk, decided I would. I had several colors to choose from in the RV, but I had grabbed a bottle of purple, so that was my hair color after getting cleaned up. I felt almost presentable after a trying day.

One thing that always came with me, in the RV or if I stayed a night elsewhere, was my sleeping bag. I could tuck the dogs in with me, and even if our world was no bigger than that insulated wrap of comfort, we were okay. It meant protection and solace. I still have it even though the filling has lumped and flattened. I haven't been able to part with this old friend that, like a tattered but cherished blankie, must always remain at hand.

I spread the sleeping bag over the motel quilt and tucked in with the dogs. We shared our customary evening snack while I narrated the "story" of our day—they love it and pay rapt attention. They recognize many of the words such as "walk," "leashes," "dog dinner," "story," "cheese snack" and many others relevant to them. They are thrilled to be included in the conversation and delight in the familiarity of words. When they were puppies, I discovered that they liked to be sung to, so I made up songs which they recognize as particular to each of them.

Magic is a gentle soul who likes baby games and nursery rhymes. I got him as a rescue at nine months old from where he had been enclosed in a pen with older, larger dogs that habitually muscled him out of meager rations. He was thin, malnourished, and had never been out of that pen. He regarded dogs and humans as unreliable and threatening—it took me an hour of patiently sitting in the pen before I could approach him. He had spent so much time hiding in a hole he had dug for protection that his ligaments had shortened and he was permanently curled in a hole-shaped posture.

It took years to repair his physical handicaps (he had lost all his front teeth and had trouble walking), for him to understand play and to trust people and other dogs. Cricket is too confident and aggressive with him, so I am Magic's safe harbor and he rarely leaves my side.

Magic's Song

Patty cake, patty cake,
Baker's man,
Bake me a cake as fast as you can—
'Cus he's a snort'n boy,
And he's a Magic Man.
Yes he is, yes he is, yes he is.

Cricket is the opposite. She's exuberant, outgoing, and deviously clever. She demands attention and insists on routine. If dinner is late, she barks and pokes at me until she's fed. And once she has a routine enforced, she'll add further requirements. Not only does she demand her favorite foods, she will pout until I cut it up for her. I go along with this; I spoil the dogs, I know.

Cricket's Song
(sung in a slightly mocking manner)

She lives by the seaside,
She longs for a boat ride,
Cricket, the dog who wants love.

As shadows grow longer,
She sits by the water,
Cricket, the dog who wants love.

As starlight is gleaming,
This dog is dog dreaming,
Cricket, the dog who wants love.

As dawn light is breaking,
Her heart is still aching,
Cricket the dog who wants love.

The word "love" is emphasized in the
performance, and at every repeat Cricket would
push closer and bury her head in my lap, while
coyly displaying her dog grin. Both dogs
understand the words "love" and "hugs" as they
are the most important aspects of our relationship.

The next morning I headed for Frazier's RV service, and it was one of the most fortuitous things to happen in my whole trip. Keith was welcoming and friendly as he introduced me to his two teenage daughters, his wife, and various dogs running around the property. Keith sized me up immediately. He figured I was stressed and not too knowledgeable, so he sent me off on a walk with Cricket and Magic while he evaluated the RV to determine why, even with a new battery from the Starter Store, my generator wasn't responding.

When I came back a half hour later, everything was working. Keith had gone over the whole RV, testing the simple stuff first while not jumping to the conclusion that if a generator won't start, it's a generator problem. He noticed that the valve for the propane feed was off. As soon as he turned the valve switch, everything worked. I hadn't thought to check when the station fellows filled the propane tank the day before. They had shut it off to fill the tank but never turned it back on.

I couldn't blame the starter service guys for not thinking of this. Their business was focused on starters. They weren't RV service people, and they didn't know I had filled the propane tank earlier in the day. I thanked them in my mind for steering me to Keith, who had professional training in RV mechanisms. Later Keith gave me a tour of my RV, teaching me how the systems worked and interacted with each other. It was the first day I felt as if I understood the RV and was confident of Keith's skills. I arranged to have parts shipped to him that he would install when I returned in the spring.

Good RV service people are hard to find. Most of them know one thing reasonably well, but not enough about all the systems, their infinite variations, and how a traveling lifestyle can make things go wrong. Even though they charge you for diagnostic time, their analytical abilities may be limited. In the big chain RV stores, if the guy out front says someone has come in with a generator not starting, they will probably assume it's the generator. The mechanic who does the work has only what was passed to him as the complaint. Work is done while you sit in the waiting room or come back another day.

With Keith, I could follow him through his diagnosis of the problem and elimination of the simple things first. This was invaluable, and I saved all my serious repairs for Keith to do for the next three years. He and his family are still my friends.

I was renewed and relaxed with better knowledge to help me keep the systems going in my motorized home. Look for RVIA (RV Industry Association) certification when you search for an RV repair person. It will save you money in the long run, eliminate the aggravation of having the same problem fixed repeatedly and most likely affect how long you remain an RVer. It will certainly make you happier. A misconception I had before my trip was that all RV owners and travelers knew what they were doing. But beware of their advice and don't let them at your rig unless you're confident in their ability.

RV components and systems aren't universal. How your neighbor's RV operates is not necessarily how things work in your rig. Advice such as "be sure and add water to your battery" only applies to lead-acid types. Messing with your AGM battery is never necessary. People who offer such repair and maintenance suggestions are no doubt amiable people wanting to be helpful. Get to know them, share a friendly glass of wine. But for good advice, find a knowledgeable, RVDA-RVIA certified technician. Spend time with them, ask about their expertise, and ask to watch the work being done. Ladies, if they patronize you and don't share information because they think you won't understand, or they don't want to take the time to explain, you have the wrong repair guy. Single women or those who have lost a partner may not think they can learn, but with effort and the right support, they surely can.

A final note on rig repairs. An RV repair person understands that it's a house with an engine, and a whole complex of issues that can go wrong in between. One of my early discoveries was the house appliances stopped working because a faulty wire on the dashboard radio was draining the battery. I tried to convince a garage mechanic that this was the problem and asked him to look at it, but he replied he didn't think so and refused to consider it. So I finally located the faulty wire and disconnected it myself. Problem solved, sort of. It no longer drained the battery—but I had no radio for three years. It wasn't essential so I let it go, instead congratulating myself for solving an immediate problem on my minimalist budget.

Toward the end of my saga, while coming back from my winter months in the south, the generator gave me trouble again. Gradually over two months it would fail to start more and more often. Knowing what I did about finding the right person, I drove three hundred miles to keep an appointment with an RV professional who had an independent business. No fancy shop, he ran his enterprise from a truck he drove for house calls, but he was RVIA certified and had been in business for thirty years. When I queried him on the phone, he was forthcoming about his particular expertise and what issues he was best at solving.

This fellow sought a remote life, living as he did deep in the isles of Lake Champlain. I drove into his yard with farmhouse, barn, and quiet beauty all around. He was a bigger man and older than Keith, but he had the same intent focus when it came to the RV. After listening to me and flipping a few switches, he crawled under the back of the RV and asked me to fetch a tiny rod from his workshop in the barn. He poked at something for a few minutes, went back to hit the generator switch, and it started with no problem. He looked up from where he was on the ground and said,

"Wasps. Mud wasp nest blocking the generator intake hose. Happens all the time with these rigs. Wasps love the smell of propane." I wonder how many people have paid for a new generator when all they needed was to clean out the intake hose.

The South

Still in North Carolina, I planned a stop-over to see my brother Bill, his sweet wife Candy, my niece Melissa whom I hadn't seen since she was a little girl, her cool husband Joe, and their two boys. The RV was perfect for a quick, informal, no-fuss visit. There was no plane or train to schedule, no long dash across several states, no set time to pick me up at the bus station or airport. No need to put me up, change plans, or arrange a full day of sightseeing. I would be at Walmart catching up on my chores, then come over for dinner. The last day of my visit, the boys stopped by the RV to see my road house and play with the dogs. Hugs for everyone, and then I was off.

This stop-over visiting with family and friends was the highlight of my years on the road. I would visit on the way south and then again on my return north. Conversation went from the big topics about politics and weddings, to how kids were doing in school, their current likes, the family dogs and cats, the crazy neighbors—the little things that make up the days. A casual visit meant less time spent on tours and events, more time renewing friend and family bonds. Those bonds cost nothing, take up no space, and can be carried with you everywhere. It was the most successful part of the trip, well worth the nights spent in Walmart parking lots.

On my first trip south I traveled farther inland than in later travels. I drove along the Blue Ridge, and having experienced those steep, narrow, and winding roads I can say I will never drive them again in an RV. By now I thought of myself as the dimensions and weight of the house I dragged behind me. I felt the momentum and constantly envisioned the possibility of all those tons careening off the road. Side roads and spectator outlooks were lovely and I drove slowly, but mostly I saw myself plunging into the spectacular drop-off along the edge.

There were places I wanted to see, a few things I thought I would do. But most tourist attractions were too expensive for my budget or of no interest. I stopped by Pedro's South of the Border in South Carolina since my Facebook friends insisted it was a right of passage for travelers. For those who haven't heard of it, South of the Border in Dillon, SC, is a Mexican-inspired attraction with gift shops and campsites off I-95.

It was a chilly twenty degrees and the parking lots were mostly bare when I arrived in the bleakness of early February. But it was on my way, so I checked out the gift shop with beaded snake-skin belts, Mexican hats, and plastic alligators. I bought a hot dog and took a picture of the dogs in front of Pedro's brightly colored, grinning statue. It's like Perry's Nut House in Belfast, Maine, or Wall Drug Store in South Dakota—one has to stop at these classic roadside attractions and maybe buy a bumper sticker to prove you've been there. Then we drove on to the next Walmart.

Being single changes an adventure. Most entertainment and attractions are for couples or groups. A big part of the experience are the reactions and comments of companions who share the adventure. The dogs were ample company, but they were mostly interested in what I was eating or when we'd take the next walk. A single person, a woman especially, is often out of place. Single RVers usually find travel companions of similar interests and budget to take in the sights. But I was on a different mission. I was reconnecting, building confidence in my capabilities, and clearing my mind. I was building an independent lifestyle that tested my strengths and ingenuity and that allowed my thoughts to wander unencumbered wherever I pleased.

Besides locating propane, there was the daily search for Wi-Fi. Whenever connected to the Internet, I spent hours studying up on solar panels, RV maintenance, and whatever would make my nomadic lifestyle sustainable. I researched the topics that Keith had alerted me to, scoured bulletin boards for RV solar panel discussions, and carefully read through suggestions for the right installation person. One name came kept coming up with comments such as "Testy, difficult personality, but the best guy for the job, really knows what he's doing." Like a hound on the scent, I fixed on a man and a place in Florida.

It continued to be freezing cold as I slipped

from South Carolina into Georgia. Beltways were my least favorite driving challenge, and the Atlanta beltway was the worst, packed with hurrying truck drivers and commuters who knew their route and the exits—which I did not. My GPS gave me suggestions of right lane or left, but there were so many lanes and so many turnoffs. Miles of space-pinching jersey barriers constrained my bulky RV to the point where I felt I should hold my breath to squeeze through. I swore I would never take that route again, and I didn't.

My experience of the South Georgia roadway was trucks, trucks, and more trucks. I suspect they haul southern fruit—oranges and peaches and whatever else—to markets farther north and west. Near the Florida border, I drove through miles of roadside truck stops and fast-food joints. Sexual "expos" and paraphernalia were heavily advertised in a massive cloud of billboards. Just on the other side of this billboard bloom, I found an open campground and by then I needed a break and a reason to get off that highway.

I pulled into an out-of-the-way place with a small pond and a large adjoining field to walk through and shake off the miles. A pleasant attendant helped me set up and connect the water hose. That night was uneventful, but the relentless cold that had followed me all the way from Massachusetts froze the water hose fitting overnight. The next morning, I wrapped up in my heavy winter coat as usual and before I could leave spent half an hour with a hair dryer to defrost and finally disconnect the fitting.

By limiting my daily miles and stopping for visits, it had taken me over a month to reach the Florida border. The panhandle of northern Florida feels the chilly breath of a continental winter, but it was finally above freezing at night. I headed toward a small town near Lake City and a man I understood was the best at RV solar panel installation. He was the only one without a negative technical review, personality aside.

I kicked my six-wheeled beast awake, pointed the diesel nose in that direction, and covered the last few miles. I found a campsite with an available spot and settled in near the Suwannee River. I parked my RV in the designated place and explored the campsite area. The river was a short walk away, and while I sat on the riverbank, the dogs stretched their legs and delighted in freedom.

The river flowed slow and calm as tree branches with long wisps of Spanish moss swayed over the unhurried water. For the moment, the stress of weather and travel slipped away.

This campground offered a clubhouse, washing machines, and showers. There was even a large sink where I could wash the dogs, and during the pleasantly warm afternoon I did. I made good use of the amenities, but encountered a lifestyle that wasn't me. Camp regulars spent days hanging out in lounge chairs next to their rigs or playing cards in the clubhouse. Scheduled events were karaoke and pot-luck suppers. Beer and wine came out at four o'clock and the chatter swelled until camp residents retired for the night. I felt like an odd person out, too restless, introverted, and reflective for this crowd. The lovely setting provided much needed respite, but the social scene didn't fit.

I looked up the mystery man who was so highly regarded in the business of solar panel installation. To my surprise, his website was the crudest I had ever seen, and anyone interested in his services was encouraged to phone since he seldom checked his email. This might seem like a poor advertisement for technical work, but I had spent half a lifetime in technical jobs and knew not to judge a book by its cover.

I would hire someone wearing a clown suit if I thought he could do the job. I actually once met a brilliant mathematician whose clothes resembled a clown suit, and I was familiar with exceptional programmers who didn't wear shoes. Eccentricity is overlooked in technical people who excel at their tasks. I called, and he assured me he'd be over to find me the next day. I had the feeling it would be like meeting Oz as I only knew him by reputation and still didn't know his exact location. It seemed he had to meet you first to see if you'd be a fit for his personality and his services. As it turned out, he lived near the campground on the other side of a small woods, but one had to meet his approval before being invited to his lair.

Every comment about him mentioned two things—his gruff personality and the excellence of his work. If you could put up with the first one, you'd get the second. He was nice enough when he came by the next morning. Bob was a large man with a commanding, booming voice. He listened carefully to what I wanted and expected, although he had solid ideas of his own. We passed the interview with each other, and the following day I arrived at his encampment in the woods.

Bob pointed out an extensive workshop, his RV, and another camper inhabited by his girlfriend. We toured several sheds full of solar panel equipment. I saw the materials he recommended and used and got explanations as to why he favored them. Clearly, I would need a lot more than solar panels. I'd need an inverter that could handle my expectations, a bank of the right batteries, and connections that allowed the setup to function at full capacity. Bob could supply and install it all—it's the only kind of work he did. He also suggested a far more efficient heating arrangement, and overall he was making good technical sense.

Bob imparted a wealth of solar power knowledge. I learned that better solar panels and more installation space on the roof means more solar energy can be gathered. But that's like money in the bank without access to the account. I also needed a well-made wiring system, several slow charge/discharge batteries, and a quality inverter. Bob suggested a $1,350 Magnum Sine Wave inverter to complete the system.

The most useful advice I could give anyone is to ask the right questions. I asked about the outcome and avoided getting overly distracted by specs. It's the whole system and how it's constructed that matters. I pressed Bob regarding appliances the completed system would run, for how long, and under what conditions. I didn't want to be disappointed when it was time to pay the bill.

Bob went over every detail of what my needs should be. Besides the solar for electric power, he suggested an improved system for extra propane and heating. He had lived and boondocked sustainably in an RV for thirty years, so he understood the requirements and possibilities for gypsy living. Along the way he had learned the skills for creating a first-rate solar system. He sketched a list of supplies needed and their costs on a small yellow tablet. It was a complete setup for efficient solar electric power and propane heat on a slip of yellow note paper. But it was good, very good.

I thanked Bob for his time and said I'd be in touch. I needed to research every item he had listed and to convince myself that I had found the right person to do the work. He said the installation would take a week, and that I could park at his woodland shop for the duration. I could observe the work and ask questions. This sounded helpful and appealing, and he would do it within my budget. The only caveat was my dogs avoided him rather than greeting him in their usual friendly way. I took note of their opinion that Bob was better avoided.

My focus shifted. My trial by polar cold melted away as I lazed my way farther south. Searching for RV services and fuel was replaced with research on Bob's solar and heat proposal. The upgrade in my systems would take most of my savings, so I had to believe I was spending it wisely. I could avoid the forty dollars a night at campgrounds, but only if the solar and heat system improvements worked and fully handled the job. I spent hours every day searching, learning, reading, studying, comparing, and figuring.

Florida is a strange place. It's a long, flat, sandbar sticking off the southern tip of the US. Once you leave northern Florida, it's a variety of cultures and climates. The dry, deserted interior of farmland is sandwiched between lively and expensive coastal cities and the idyllic offshore islands.

The woodlands are different, especially if there is water. A stand of pine trees suddenly becomes an overgrown tangle of vines that's impossible to walk through, and solid ground gives way to just enough water to fill your shoes. Pockets of deeper water hide alligators that, to my surprise, showed up everywhere. So instead of investigating the wild areas I stopped at a gift shop, bought six T-shirts with imprints of alligators, and shipped them to my grandchildren.

I stopped in Sarasota to reconnect with my college friend, Andy, and her husband Dan. I hadn't seen Andy for fifty years, since college, but we picked up right where we left off. Dan was funny and mused that the fun of visiting them was because they were such wonderful people—haha —and that was true. Andy's brother took me on a tour of the Ringling Museum. We toured the magnificent art collection, lovely grounds, and a spectacular miniature circus that filled an immense room. The visit was topped off with a day in the orchid gardens with Andy.

I made for the Florida interior and another acquaintance I'd met through our newly discovered RV living. Louise was helpful with suggestions, such as her recommendation to invest in a good RV GPS. I caught up with her in a long-term RV campground in the midlands. There was nothing else for miles. It was inexpensive to park there since there was no other reason to be in that place, but Louise was energetic and didn't mind driving hundreds of miles a day to seek out amusements. She had found like-minded friends, and they enjoyed attending week-long seminars and touring attractions together. They pursued adventure during the day and relaxed with wine in the late afternoon. It suited them perfectly, happily. Year-round residents watched TV and planned golf cart races for the weekends.

Louise was fun and helpful—she did a sewing job for me—but it wasn't enough to keep me there for long. I had been on so many tours, taken classes, and attended social gatherings that I didn't need anymore. I enjoyed Bluegrass but would rather have been at Tanglewood and wasn't into line dancing. Golf cart races were not my thing. I liked hiking and trails and walking with my dogs, but Central Florida wasn't the best environment for that.

At the small pond where Louise was camped, it didn't occur to me that it would be filled with alligators. When Magic decided to go for a swim, the alarm went out and campers came rushing and screaming from everywhere. Fortunately, I still had Magic on a leash while he swam, and I yanked him from the approaching jaws of death. I learned to avoid water as invariably a few nasty reptiles eyed my dogs as if they were hamburgers.

South again, and I was in Palmdale, Florida. On the way I had avoided the larger cities like Orlando and Tampa. I thought about visiting the Everglades and a good friend at Marathon along the Keys, but I discovered the Keys are not the outposts I thought. Much is built up now, more exclusive and expensive than in the romantic past. RVs are restricted for lack of road and parking space, and parking for me would be too costly at one hundred dollars a night. I checked with a campground near Marathon, but they didn't allow dogs. I was a non-drinking single senior woman with two dogs and a cat and was sure I'd be out of place for that venue anyway. Reluctantly, I messaged my friend, Peggy, in Marathon that I wouldn't be able to come. It would have been a thousand mile trek back and forth for a two-day visit.

So far, unless I was with friends or family, I hadn't spent more than a single night in one place, mostly freezing Walmart parking lots. I had spent only a few nights at campgrounds when I was far enough south to find one open. But it was the end of February, and I found myself parked in a quiet back space at the Palmdale campground. The days were near eighty degrees, close to a hundred degrees more than when I had started. I hooked up to water and sewage, walked to the campground office, and signed up to stay for a week. I would think over my trip so far, recover from navigating the highways every day, and decide on batteries, inverters, and solar panels.

Nothing could have been better for me in Palmdale than to have Cricket and Magic. They were company during my journey, and I didn't consider my singleness an advertisement for the campground companionship that voyeurs are seeking. Most guys are gentlemen, and I met many wonderful, helpful men during my travels. I stayed in their homes without worrying about their intentions. But every so often there is a guy who takes a month-long hiatus from his wife while parked at a campground. He's prowling for female companionship, no strings attached, see you next year. I'm not interested, but that doesn't always deter the persistent sort.

While at Palmdale I met one of these fellows. First, there was a casual dinner at his place, pleasant enough, but of course I showed up with my faithful dogs. The next day he suggested I exercise the dogs to exhaustion and leave them at home while I visited him for "another relaxing dinner." The emphasis was on "relaxing." No dogs, no me. My refusal didn't stick, and he frequented my remote end of the park, circling my RV on his bike. I got the respite I needed, but was eager to leave the campground and this annoying, creepy guy by the end of the week.

During my stay, I'd had time to contemplate my financial resources. Throughout the last month of my trip south, I stopped at campgrounds to restore body, mind, and spirit. I found discounts for RV travelers, so a night might cost $15 instead of $35. But that was for one night only. The best rates targeted snowbirds who stayed through the winter and booked months in advance. I was paying up to $45 dollars for a parking spot with a hot shower, and sometimes even that was an extra cost. One campground required a quarter for every thirty seconds of shower water. I recall being thoroughly soaped up, hair full of shampoo, naked, fishing through my pocketbook for one more quarter so I could rinse off.

Back in Sarasota, I spent a few return visit days with Andy and Dan. We reminisced about college and old friends. I walked the dogs along the development's winding park-like roads, while still breathing sighs of relief that I had finally escaped snowstorms and frigid weather.

I made a point to stop in Homosassa where I joined a tour group that swam with manatees. I spent half an hour freezing in the unusually cold coastal water, but I did get to pat one of those amazing creatures. I'm glad I made the side trip, but that night I appreciated warming up in the sleeping bag with the dogs and crossed "swim with manatees" off my bucket list.

Solar Panels

Bob's proposal in hand, I went over everything I had researched about solar panels, batteries, and inverters and made the decision that I'd have Bob do the job. I called him, scheduled a date, and started back toward the Suwannee.

When I arrived, I went directly to Bob's shop in the woods instead of the nearby campground. Bob welcomed me warmly enough and introduced me to his young apprentice who would assist with the installation. It would take the two of them a week to complete the work.

During the first few days, they secured four one-hundred watt panels to the roof while I cleared out my outside storage compartments. I would need the additional propane tanks more than the sundry items stored there. I suspected I wouldn't be needing the beach chairs, fishing poles, and large cooking pots for forty people. Instead, a new bank of four AGM batteries replaced the lead-acid battery I had purchased at the Starters place in North Carolina, and a Magnum Sine Wave inverter filled a separate compartment of its own. I cleared another compartment that would hold the two extra propane tanks. Inside the RV, I made space for a small propane heater which I was assured would be worth it, and in time it surely was.

The workshop and encampment were located in a woods with wonderful trails that looked like a setting from *Lord of the Rings*. There were tortoise burrows and a cacophony of birdsong. The dogs raced free along over a mile of footpaths and I enjoyed the downtime in the woods along the river.

Back at the RV, I watched the guys cut thick, pure copper wire and I appreciated its quality. I was paying thousands, but suspected it could cost twice as much for a job done half as well. I didn't regret my decision to have the solar installation done under Bob's auspices.

The work was good, but the warnings about Bob's behavior were equally reliable. The property

Bob rented belonged to an elderly couple who appeared to be traveling the long, sad, road into dementia. Bob was not kind to them—he was controlling and verbally abusive. Every time he encountered his frail landlords, he raised his voice and a torrent of unjustifiable expletives would follow. He towered, red-faced and angry, over his innocent victims until dazed and befuddled, they wandered away.

After witnessing this behavior a few times, I avoided him except to go over the installation progress. I was out in the woods more often with the dogs and sequestered inside the RV when we returned. Most people would knock first, but toward the end Bob just came bursting in to deliver a diatribe of his concerns, most often about his hapless landlords. I felt sorry for the senile but sweet couple and hoped the work would finish before I went from a valued customer to another target of Bob's belligerence.

Bob and his helper completed the work on the sixth day, so it was time for the final run-through. Almost everything was able to run on solar except the air conditioning, and it was unrealistic to think that it would. But I could run lights, my computer, the refrigerator, and especially the microwave. I felt great about the propane heater and solar setup, but I was uneasy with Bob's behavior.

That afternoon Bob came booming through the door, highly upset about whatever, when my alarmed dogs raced by him out the door. They were off barking, the resident chickens scattered, and I was pinned in the RV while Bob continued to explode in a tirade that now included invectives about me. I finally got past him to chase after the dogs and corral them back to the RV, although they were reluctant to be in the same space as this menacing despot, and I sympathized. Bob had been paid, and I knew enough about the solar installation to run it confidently, so without a goodbye, I was off early the next morning. I was shaken, but I had been warned. Bob does the best work, but at the price of putting up with his belligerent manner.

I found a Walmart for the night and reluctantly abandoned my hope of visiting my childhood friend, Susan, in Texas. I would have loved to reminisce about our childhood growing up in upstate New York, the neighborhood gang of kids, the day we powdered her mother's bathroom, and the walkie-talkie we strung across the road that attracted a police cruiser as it slowly sagged onto the asphalt. But I had learned the expense and effort for each mile requiring diesel and propane, and Texas appeared even larger than I had imagined. Instead, I checked my notes on each stop along my way south and planned a reverse course making the same stops back up the coast. I hoped spring weather would follow me.

Walmart by Walmart, I went northward through Georgia while avoiding Atlanta and its nightmare beltway. I passed Pedro's South of the Border in South Carolina but didn't stop. Every evening was a one-nighter until I was back in North Carolina visiting my brother Bill and his family again.

Bob's propane heater and solar electric power was proving well worth the coast. My use of propane for heat had declined markedly. I stayed comfortable with the small interior heater on the coldest nights and during the day I did fine with just the pilot running. There was less noise and rumble of the generator starting up every few hours, and I could use the microwave for short periods without turning the "genny" on at all. The old sleeping bag tucked around my back bedroom window kept it dark but cozy. The dogs, Milo, and I hunkered down in our safe and sheltered hide-away.

I was relieved to have better systems running and congratulated myself on the decision to approve the installations. I had studied unfamiliar mechanics and made my choices. There had been no one else to commiserate with, and I'd summoned my abilities and strengths in getting the RV outfitted for my lifestyle. I didn't regret my solo adventure as Cricket, Magic, and Milo were exemplary comrades, and I was fine with myself for human company. I engaged my mind and acquired knowledge. My journey was a quest for self-confidence, a quiet mind, and a peaceful soul, and I was getting there. I took my time as I wandered the roads, since my destination wasn't a place but rather a state of mind.

Back in North Carolina, I kept my appointment with Keith and had more work done. All the replacement pieces I'd ordered had arrived. Keith installed a new chair to replace the one that was falling apart, located and fixed a leak in the propane line, repaired dents and rust areas, replaced a broken taillight, and overall had things looking good and working well. I enjoyed time with the whole family, joining them for dinners, and meeting Grandma while admiring her craft skills. I promised to visit on return trips south since surely I'd accumulate more repairs needing attention. My last night there I studied maps and weather predictions in the hope of finishing my trip back north just behind the melting snows of spring.

Virginia was uneventful, but it snowed again when I reached Maryland for a return stay with Kathy and Al. I was cruising slowly, as usual, and took note of unexpected heavy drifting across the country roads. A tractor-trailer hadn't, and he jackknifed just a few minutes before I arrived. He was stuck with each end of the truck hanging off opposite sides of the road. A single cop had just arrived, and I was the first to be told to turn around and go back. I had to back up in a yard meant only for cars, and by some miracle I didn't take out their stone wall and garden. When I got to Kathy's house it snowed again.

There was our usual chatter and Kathy's outstanding meals. One topic was of GPS systems that allow friends and family to access a map indicating the traveler's whereabouts, updated every two hours. Kathy and Al had it for their boat trips, and it was reassuring and fun to follow a friend's daily progress. However, we agreed that a daily track of my travels wasn't so reassuring since I roamed everywhere, seemingly without a plan or reason.

I had briefly borrowed their device and besides my meandering random back roads, it had been alarming when one night it traced a frenetic pattern all over a Walmart parking lot. It's only accurate to so many feet, so I appeared to be wandering through the night from one corner of the lot to another, each spot about ten-to-twenty feet from the previous location. We decided that it might be interesting if I slapped the GPS tracker on an eighteen-wheeler truck headed to California. My trip voyeurs would see a digital map of me helplessly staggering around a parking lot all night and then—wow—I'd be charging across the country at warp speed. I'm still laughing.

I had been meeting friends online and decided I would detour far to the west of my Allentown Walmart. I crossed the mountains to State College, Pennsylvania, found my new friend, Sharon (a relation to Margaret in Salem), and by some miracle her gate opening had clearance no wider than the thickness of paint for my RV to slip through. I stayed a day, had a wonderful time, but will pass on repeating that trip in an RV. The mountains were horrendous with steep grades and terrifying drop-offs for miles. Trucks traveled these roads, but their maximum speed was limited to twenty-five miles an hour. I don't think I went over fifteen the whole way.

The travel arc rounding New York City always seemed tediously long. Then a stop in Danbury, Connecticut, where it was as friendly as ever. A few more stops, a few more nights in Walmart parking lots, and I was back in Massachusetts. Snow lingered, but it was piled in great mountains along the edges of parking lots. Spring was winning against the retreating winter.

Summer in Salem

I'd completed my winter traveling south. I had
visited friends, caught up with family, and
upgraded the RV for more sustainable living. It
took effort, tested my endurance, and cost money,
but I was feeling "what doesn't kill you makes you
stronger." Late spring, summer, and early fall—the
next several months—would be house-sitting in
Salem for Margaret. She had an industrial RV that
would climb mountains and ford streams, liked to
take extended travel, and wanted her freedom. I
was girl Friday when she was home, and house-
sitter when she traveled. I had a place to rest and
collect my thoughts.

I had much to catch up on, including neglected
paperwork. I had registered the RV in
Massachusetts because of my connections, but I

didn't have an acceptable location for the authorities. They prefer to know you're locked in place, living in a house or apartment, so they always know where to find you. I was able to claim I was 'living' at a UPS post office box number that, for a few extra dollars, appeared as a physical address. I picked up my packages that had been delivered there, paid an excise tax at Salem City Hall, and shored up my claim as a resident.

My only glitch was the RV registration. I assumed it was like cars, renewable each year on the same date. Not so for RVs. They are considered summer vehicles, and all registrations expire in November. I had registered just two weeks before the end date, so became technically unregistered two weeks later. I was so stunned by the amount of the excise tax that I hadn't noticed, and since the UPS store manager had forwarded little of my mail, I missed the notices on lapsed registration and the rescinding of my vehicle insurance. I had been driving for my whole trip south and back unregistered and uninsured. Fortunately, I'm a conservative driver and just plain lucky.

I had been cloistered in my own mental space

for months, and suddenly it was like the power coming back after days of blackout. The lights were on, and it was noisy and chaotic. Instead of pacing my days, I was back in the frenzy with everyone else, hurrying from one errand to the next, making phone calls, and setting up appointments for this or that.

Functionaries abhor a wanderer. Without a fixed address, one is suspect. I had been fortunate to get the RV registration with only a post office box number (the box number becomes your street number), and it helped that my driver's license was issued with the same. The insurance that I was reestablishing hassled me since the box number bounced in their system. The questions came over and over: "But where do you *park*?" "Where do you *stay*?" "What trailer park do you live in?" I understand they need to calculate their actuarial figures, and that I lived where I happened to be on any given night would not do.

I felt minimal administrative hounding while on the road, and I liked it that way. I resented that a recent utility bill or a note from a landlord legitimized me as an upstanding citizen. Owning an RV for recreation indicates solid middle-class status, but living in one is another matter. Without a record of payments attached to a location, you are disconnected trailer trash that should be moved along. Like so many others, I learned to move frequently on city streets and never stayed at a Walmart or Lowe's parking lot more than a day or two. I was parked in Margaret's driveway, but town ordinances prohibited that as well. The first couple of years I slipped by the rules, but eventually I was told that the limit was thirty days, and then I had to leave.

I completed paperwork so that by the beginning of June my insurance and registration were current. My location and identity was as fixed as I could get it to please the administrative watchdogs. I enjoyed my living space in the RV, and the solar power and the inside heater worked well. With all this in place, I was confident about traveling and staying at Walmarts again the following winter. I had excess "stuff" in a small Salem storage unit and thought long and hard about the car I'd left behind. I decided to part with anything I was unlikely to need in the next year.

Without towing a car, my twenty-seven foot RV was perfect, particularly since it was unusually narrow. I fit in most driveways and double parking spaces. I could get around town with little trouble, and my RV amazed me at how it turned on a dime. The biggest advantage was, hands down, that I could back up without jackknifing a towed vehicle. I had no car to connect and disconnect or to check for backup lights. I didn't have to worry about vehicles I couldn't see behind the towed car. So I sold the car and pocketed a little more money to take south with me the following winter.

I was relinquishing accumulations of stuff, the car, and a lot of mental baggage. By mid-summer, the whirlwind of catching up had settled and I spent whole days in Margaret's backyard overlooking an ocean cove. The only thing I missed was my own land to cultivate, but I made up for it by planting a small strip of garden along the shore and weeding Margaret's overgrown landscape. I walked with the dogs, and the daily routine was pleasant and easy until I met the critter that would be my nemesis for the rest of my days in Salem.

While rambling in a vacant woodlot next to Margaret's neighborhood, I noticed a large coyote-looking creature shadowing us on occasion. He'd follow us several yards behind, and if I stopped, he'd stand and stare at me—and especially the dogs. I later learned that it was a newly recognized urban animal, a wolf-coyote hybrid called a coywolf. I misinterpreted its behavior as curious and friendly, but after some experience with this critter, I learned that what I understood as benign interest from this fifty-pound predator was in fact stalking. He was waiting for his chance to grab my yummy dogs.

The media echos the opinion of most wildlife officials that the coywolf is a harmless creature of nature returning to its native habitat taken over by human encroachment. Not quite so. They are a new form of canid that has evolved and adapted to urban living. They often hunt alone, don't fear people, invade backyards, and have been known to enter houses and garages that have been left open. They live on what's available in urban and residential settings, i.e., garbage, compost, and small pets. Their dens are littered with collars and ID tags of unfortunate cats and dogs who have fallen prey. Most prefer not to interact with people, but the one that stalked my dogs and me had a definite plan in mind.

One day he made his move and grabbed Cricket, who lagged a few feet behind me. Magic exploded like a hand grenade on the coywolf, who was stunned that a dog the size of a meatloaf would take him on. The astounded coywolf dropped Cricket, who was screaming in pain and horror. He had bitten her within an inch of her spine.

The coywolf had tasted blood and continued to stalk us for the rest of the summer. It hid under the RV or Margaret's porch and followed us every day from the time we stepped out the door. Three pups grew up in the little nearby woods that summer, and the gang of them marauded around the neighborhood. Some nights they joined in a howl fest in the middle of the road. A neighbor with a disabled child no longer left her daughter unattended in her yard. Beloved dogs and cats went missing.

Even when the coywolf family wasn't close, I could see them on the beach across the cove sitting just below the tangle of bushes and vines, watching us, waiting for an inattentive moment to finish the attack on Cricket. I am a nature lover, but I felt persecuted by this coywolf and lost sympathy for his kind.

Then it was late summer, early fall—that glorious, wonderful season with the sunset golden on the harbor waters. Being so near the water created the impression of living on a boat. Actually, in many ways living in an RV is like living aboard. I had spent time on boats before and it prepared me for living with far fewer things and enjoying it. For every item gone, there is less responsibility, less to take care of. Everything is downsized in the RV, but when I stepped out the door, it was like living in all outdoors.

Making Another Plan

I was much better prepared than the year before, but I needed a new plan for the winter travel. I'd make some of the same stops with family and friends. Arriving in the RV made me an easy guest, but I'd limit my stays so I'd be welcome again. For several weeks of my previous trip south, I stayed on the property of the repair and installation guys, but that work was done. I had splurged on a month's worth of nights at campgrounds, but with the solar power working so well that strain on my budget shouldn't be necessary. I would have many nights at Walmart, but I needed a goal, a mission, for my second year.

I didn't feel at home in the campgrounds. I wasn't going on vacation and had little money to spare beyond necessities. I hadn't made fast friends at campsites and didn't think I'd find common ground at rallies where the camaraderie is based on what kind of RV one owns. I was happy with my choice of RV, but I had made it for practical reasons, not with a vision of an owner's jamboree. I was reuniting with old friends and distant family, which was more to my liking.

Otherwise, I was more interested in getting to know the local towns and people than in roadside attractions or campground socializing. Spending an afternoon in a Walmart parking lot wasn't promising as a social event, but it had its merits. I'd walk the dogs on arrival at the next Walmart stop, and they attracted enough attention to suffice for daily socializing on the road. I could shop for dinner with no need to plan ahead for a stay at a campground—if I forgot butter or ran out of cooking oil, it was a short walk across the parking lot. There was Wi-Fi streaming if I could get it and the latest DVDs at Redbox or books if I couldn't.

My afternoons were filled with a marathon of documentaries on economic, historical, or social commentary topics, along with investigative reports from *Al Jazeera* or *PBS Frontline*. Other days I went on virtual expeditions to explore distant jungles, trek across deserts, or climb mountain peaks. I spent countless hours digesting the history and politics of finance, the impetus behind wars and migrations, and the inspiration behind social movements. Online information is remarkably vast, and I was delighted to have the uninterrupted time to study and process.

But Walmart was for a night or two, and it didn't connect me with local culture or history. The internet came to the rescue again as I found house-and pet-sitting opportunities for which I was well suited. After landing at my daily Walmart stop, I'd plan distances and stops for the next day, then check for the latest house-sitting opportunities in the direction I was headed. If I got a hit, I'd email my introductions and qualifications. Although I hadn't connected with the campgrounds, living among locals was a perfect fit, and I got to know my hosts in the days before and after their trips. I met interesting people, slipped comfortably into their neighborhoods, and made fast friends with people I've stayed in touch with long after my trip.

By September, I had arranged for my first house-sitting job. I would leave Salem at the end of October, which would be a less desperate departure than last January. I had functioning solar panels, so even in Walmart parking lots I would have power without hookup cost or constantly searching for propane. I was more aware of possible perils, but more confident in my ability to handle them.

I have been asked how I managed aspects of my driving venture such as high-rise bridges, since everyone knew I feared heights. Maybe it's my age. At some point, advancing age excuses its victim from further effort. You're done, it's time to let go, retire, take it easy. But in my case, I decided it was time to let nothing hold me back, including the fears I carried in my own head.

In my later sixties, I joined a volunteer crew on a replica tall ship moored in Salem Harbor. Many crew members were retirees with the time and attitude to engage fully in this challenging physical, mental, and social enterprise. With them as inspiration, I decided I could qualify to climb the rigging. I rowed daily to build up strength, and on the day of the test I looked up the ropes and went. It was terrifying to climb the futtock shrouds, the ropes one climbs to reach the platform (the "top") fifty-six feet above the deck. The secret is to understand that the time to accomplish anything on this planet is winding down. Your ending won't be any different, only what you did.

I learned that I could do what I put my mind to, and a year later, on my sixty-eighth birthday, I achieved my open water (ocean) diving certificate. A distant hurricane was impacting coastal waters, so twenty feet down in churning, murky, water I turned blue with cold that day late in October. But I had learned to apply willpower to any physical strength I could muster. The only thing I could see was the rope to the surface, so I focused on that lifeline while waiting for the instructor to put me through my paces. A key test is to remove one's mask, replace and clear it of water while unable to see anything. The experience was trying, but it was another accomplishment. In ways this trip was the same. I was mustering my courage, exploring, and discovering what I could do.

By the beginning of November, I was on the road heading to southern states again. The first night I went no further than the Walmart stop in Worcester, just west of Boston, while the dogs, Milo, and I reacquainted ourselves with the routine of daily travel.

By driving short distances between daily stops, I increased my days of free parking. My immediate goal was to head south and west while avoiding Hartford, New York City, and Philadelphia. It was a long way around the coastal cities, staying to the west of them while at the same time avoiding the mountains—the Catskills and the long arm of the Appalachians. I went through Windsor Locks, Waterbury, and Danbury, Connecticut. Then Middletown, New York, Allentown and Lancaster, Pennsylvania, with an overnight in a Walmart parking lot in each. I spent a night in York with the memories of nearly freezing to death except for my candles the year before. I was doing infinitely better.

Every stop was a Walmart Supercenter, open twenty-four hours, with lights in the parking lot, night-shift shoppers, surveillance cameras, and hopefully somewhere a guard on duty. I was into gypsy living, accumulating nothing and needing little. I watched the Walmart shoppers load carts with non-essentials that would fill up their homes, then migrate to storage, and eventually contribute to landfill. I was observing this cycle in American living but didn't participate.

My mail rarely got forwarded from Salem to house-sits where I'd be for a week or more, and I became more disconnected from that home base. In a sense I was homeless, although I didn't feel that way. I just felt free from distractions, immersed in the adventure of every day.

By my second year of travel, things in the RV began to break. With little money and the fix-it people hundreds of miles away, I had to manage. When the control panel button got stuck, I dug out the screwdriver, opened the outlet cover, and dove into the panel. I unstuck the jammed button and gained confidence by succeeding in such small feats. I was the first and last solution chief for anything that became non-functioning.

I continued to dye my hair various shades of pastel blue and purple. In Salem it wasn't out of the ordinary, but when I started my trips south, I wondered how I'd be received at other places looking like a hippy grandma. To my surprise, most people liked it. I'd hear "Right on!" from the teenagers, "Go lady" from the men, and a whispered "I wish I could do that" from older women. Women should know there is nothing to stop them except your surrounding culture, your own view of yourself, and maybe frowning family members. But ultimately, most restrictions are of our own making, and I was tossing them aside every day that I traveled. I didn't get the memo about aging gracefully.

The history of my colorful hair began when I had my children. By then, my college-years strawberry blonde had faded to a drab shade with white strands. An admirer commented about my children, "What lovely hair they have! Do they get it from their father?" It sent me straight to the drug store searching for chemicals to restore my strawberry blonde, but it never quite worked. I looked as if I were wearing a single-hued helmet, and after a week it looked like a helmet with roots.

I tried for years to get it just right. Instead I had perpetual "bad hair." So I let my hair grow out to a stunning snowy white. I thought it looked good, but instead of admiration, I was suddenly viewed as "older" and "less capable." So back to the drug store, and this time I chose a magenta shade that brought cheers from my friends and high-fives from the strangers I passed on the streets of Salem.

To my surprise, expressive hair color opened

doors and invited friendly comments all along the way. There was little to distinguish me other than my blue/purple hair. Otherwise I was just jeans, T-shirt, flannel over-shirt. I could be any aging senior. If my flannel shirt looked as if it had come from Abercrombie & Fitch, it might mark me as a well-off matron who wore this shirt into my carefully maintained garden to gather entries for the garden club flower show. An L.L. Bean rugged over-shirt with an "easy fit" could peg me as an outdoor type, but would be baggy and billow beyond my slender frame as if I were sailing into old age.

Trendy REI and sports stores are pricey, so I finally found a nameless flannel shirt on eBay that would make due. I dressed anonymously with little to signal where I was from, where I was going, or what I was about. But with my roguish hair color I was most often interpreted as individualistic and open-minded. People with dogs, teenagers, those who are put upon for their color or ethnicity, and anyone who thought they were passing by life's adventures were inclined to feel comfortable and start a conversation with me. These were the people I was most interested in anyway, so that was fine. And no one had to remember my name

—I was "the lady with the purple hair" and generally regarded as socially conscious, fun, and approachable.

So I stayed with my purple or whatever hair color of the day. I have a realistic understanding of my advancing years so kept it pastel and not too outrageous, but creatively colored for the whole three years of my trip. As I aged, was I bucking the standard look and behavior expected? Was I raging against "that good night"? Probably.

In Others' Homes

In Maryland I stopped again at Kathy and Al's home in horse and farm country. This time, we picked up from where we left off only a few months before. It was the same in North Carolina with my brother and his family. Just a quick stop to visit, have dinner, spend an evening catching up on the latest dramas, vacations, or illnesses.

I moved uneventfully through Virginia and North Carolina until South Carolina, where I visited Sally. I met her online, on a Schipperke dog forum where her comical and amusing comments convinced me I'd enjoy getting to know her, so I decided to ask if I could stop by. Sally owned three Schipperkes like mine and two Australian Shepherds. A raucous greeting erupted between her five dogs and my two as I pulled up in the RV and opened my door. Schipperkes are loud, and bark when excited, but Sally and I were unaffected by their yapping and we quickly became friends.

Sally and her dogs were lively, funny, and welcoming. I arrived early in December and stayed through the first week of January. We hung out, entertained the dogs, and I did house and dog sitting for a week while Sally went house-hunting in another state. Sally shared a sense of adventure and boldly pushed her personal boundaries. She could pull up stakes to find new friends in new places if it suited her.

Sally didn't blink as I referred to myself as "we," meaning "me and the dogs." I didn't go places and do things—"we" did. "We" watched movies and had snacks. "We" had dinner. The "we" of me and the dogs was thoroughly knitted into the fabric of my day. Sally likewise had her dogs on a pedestal, and nothing was too good for them. Cricket and Magic fit right in, and when Sally went house-hunting I had the seven of them to entertain. Sally was one of the new acquaintances that became a fast friend.

When she returned, Sally gave me a tour of the Lowcountry in South Carolina that tourists miss.

We parked at the entrance of dirt roads that disappeared into a Creole wilderness. Somewhere along those roads were the Gullahs, a community that has lived there since the end of the Civil War. In these hidden neighborhoods, Gullah women weave their baskets in the style of their native African countries, the Gold Coast and Sierra-Leone, and speak a Creole language of their own.

We—that is Sally, Cricket, Magic, and I—wandered through the Lowcountry, passing through the smallest of towns and stopping at the end of long roads, each with a story to tell at the end of it. In contrast to the rural Gullah roads, we paused in front of a dramatically large iron gate guarding a refined estate. It looked equally private, but unlike the Gullah communities, it partitioned off the wealthy who arrived to hunt quail for sport. Sally explained the controversy over owls—the locals who would protect native owls locked horns with the privileged citizenry calling for their extermination, since owls prey on the stocked quail, thus ruining their hunting entertainment. As I gazed down the road behind that massive, intimidating gate, I envisioned Dick Cheney shooting Harry Whittington, and I silently cheered for the owls.

We passed through Yamessee, a small town as socially distant from a country club as one can get. It's located somewhere between Green Pond and Early Branch. I supposed there might be a Coke dispenser somewhere, but it wasn't a town you'd otherwise stop in. A partially painted building surrounded by the debris of rusting bicycles and broken window frames sat on one side of the barely paved street. In front was a mailbox that looked unused and a hand-written sign announcing the building was closed for business on Saturday. There was no indication of what that business might be.

We visited a graveyard with fresh Confederate flags on almost every grave. Here there is only one war—The War. Other wars are the business of other places. This war is held close and one could sense the angst it still evokes. The long wisps of willow tree branches that brushed the gravestones seemed to be consoling the dead. I could feel the spirits of those looking for fallen brothers or lost sons, or maybe a soldier searching for a wounded friend. As the sun settled on the horizon, I offered a silent apology for our intrusion, and we went on our way.

As we headed home, we discussed the pronunciations of Beaufort, South Carolina, and Beaufort, North Carolina. It's critically important to know that the Beaufort of South Carolina is pronounced "BYOO-fert" (as in "beautiful"). The Beaufort of coastal North Carolina is "BOH-fert" (as in "Beauregard"), which is also the correct pronunciation of the Duke of Beaufort for which it is named. Visitors had best get this memorized and quickly. The wrong pronunciation stings the locals, and the corrections won't stop until you do.

That year, the winter in South Carolina was unusually warm. Over Christmas while house-sitting at Sally's, the dogs and I stayed out of the hot sun. I organized the RV, caught up on laundry, and took time to watch the wind make ripples on swampy water at the foot of the yard while Spanish moss drifted lazy fingertips of gray-green across the grass.

By early January, Sally returned from her trip, and I prepared to go on my way. I didn't travel much farther south that year. Other than Andy and Dan in Sarasota, Florida offered little for the miles it would take to get there. Instead I stopped just south of the Georgia border before pointing the RV northward, toward home.

Extending my trip into Savannah with its particularly friendly visitor center and inexpensive RV parking at $12 a day was well worth it. It's a good walking city with squares or small parks along almost every street. The locals are outgoing and welcoming, similar to my hometown Salem people, and I met Salem people who had moved there for that reason. It was the setting for *Midnight in the Garden of Good and Evil*, a captivating story about murder and the quirky inhabitants of this city with social rules all its own. I bought the DVD in the visitor center and enjoyed being in the surroundings of that wonderful tale. Cricket, Magic, and I walked the route of the tour buses and gave Savannah an A+ evaluation.

In contrast, I'd had enough of Charlestown after a quick visit. No doubt parking in the basement of a parking garage, the only space allotted for RVs, influenced my impression. Right next to me, tour buses and local transport of all kinds belched fumes, and engines roared night and day. Much of the antebellum charm had been destroyed during the Civil War years due to a devastating fire, an unprecedented 587 days of bombardment, and by General Sherman's revenge on a city considered the instigator of rebellion when it fired on Fort Sumter. I only stayed a day, and we were back on the road.

As I left South Carolina behind, the single-and double-wide homes were fewer and rural poverty showed less. Crossroads with little more than a dollar store and a church gave way to more affluent surroundings. It amused me that the farther north I drove, a trendy interest in tiny houses infused the social consciousness. In the deep southern states "tiny houses" had clearly been standard housing for field hands or the otherwise impoverished for generations.

I revisited my brother and his family in North Carolina, then made my way to a month-long house-sit in Virginia. I landed the job because I had grown up raising poultry and was knowledgeable in its management. Besides a portly dog and an aging cockatiel, I would attend to the safety and feeding of fifty chickens and ducks. Barbara and Curtis, their owners, had named each chicken and every one of them had a significance. They especially loved a soft gray chicken named Opal, and asked that she be given special attention and care. (Years later when Opal died they were devastated, and they mourn her still.)

My job was to not only feed and care for them, but to fend off the hawks, foxes, and raccoons that were fixed on having them for a meal. Mother Nature challenged me with unusually harsh weather, and for the entire month of February, it never went above zero. Every two hours, I carried buckets of fresh, unfrozen water to the beloved poultry. Up the hill, down the hill and back again. I was earning my stay and a place to park the hard way, but I didn't lose a single chicken.

Besides the chickens, my special assignment was to provide emotional support for Floyd, their Australian Cattle Dog. The liveliness and confident nature of this breed had been undermined by his unfortunate early years. Floyd had not found a home when he was a puppy, so as the last of the litter, he was left alone and confined in a horse stall in a barn. Curtis and Barbara estimated he'd been in that solitary situation for up to five years before they brought him home.

Floyd had more than the usual dog adoration for his rescuers, especially Curtis. He wasn't outwardly demonstrative, but was always close by and would amble around the yard behind his savior. Curtis and Barbara forewarned that whenever they left, Floyd went into full separation anxiety, especially if they weren't home at night. I promised to give him particular attention.

The first night they were gone, Floyd collapsed next to my bed, shaking uncontrollably and doing what I can best describe as sobbing. There was no sleeping with a dog so distressed. I tried hanging my arm over the side of the bed and stroked poor Floyd for an hour. Finally I managed to drag his eighty pounds up onto the bed with Cricket and Magic, and somewhere late in the night we all fell asleep. The next night I got him up on the bed to start, and the four of us slept together for the month his owners were away.

As usual, it was fun to meet the homeowners and to become familiar with their community. Fredericksburg had a strong historical, but perhaps less visceral feel for the Civil War than the Carolinas, and instead it was infused with current politics because of its proximity to Washington,

DC. I stayed a week after my hosts' return, and became more integrated into Fredericksburg. I joined Barbara in flower arranging and frequented the local farm market. In the back of my mind, I penciled in Fredericksburg as a potential place to settle after my RV ventures.

As bad as February had been, March promised to turn the corner into spring. My solar panels and space heater kept me comfortable as I meandered northward from one Walmart to the next. I was less desperate to find daily propane, and didn't have to get up every two hours in the night. This year, I avoided the mountains and major cities and did less wandering on side roads. I stayed a night or maybe two at each Walmart, depending on the height of leftover snow piles. If there was enough blacktop exposed to catch and hold the warmth of daylight sun, I'd move on the next day. If it was still snow-covered and icy, I'd linger a day longer.

I was the embodiment of "slow living," disengaged from distractions, junk mail, robocalls, and anything beyond immediate RV upkeep. The only disturbance could be a knock on the door, followed by a suggestion from a parking lot attendant that I should move on. That was easily done, and another location to park was rarely more than thirty miles away.

Cocooned as I was in my own traveling tiny house, I continued to evolve. I had left behind therapists, pills to forget problems, and the promises of serenity that could be purchased for a price. Before my trip, I had spent time and money only to become dependent on an unhealthy relationship and entrenched in unhealthy patterns. I looked outward for solutions and embraced bad advice, when I should have been reaching into myself. Ultimately, I had driven away in my tiny ark to challenges unknown.

Years before, I had been intrigued by a postcard with the picture of a gnarly toad and the advice to "Eat a live toad each morning and it will be the worst thing you will have to do all day." That solemn, humorous advice I now took to heart. The discipline I learned early in my trip became routine, thoroughly ingrained in my habits, and I expanded it to anything I might consider putting off or mentally debate to the point of avoiding it altogether. Then I was free and my days were better than they had been in a long, long time.

When I pulled in at my Walmart landings, the main stress of the day was behind me. The relief when I'd stop was a daily celebration. "We're here, dogs, we're here at Walmart!" (In the language they understood, I pronounced it something like "Waamowt, Waamowt!") I delighted in the simplest things—a good place to park near Wi-Fi, a place to walk the dogs, enough solar power for the microwave, and a hot dinner.

In a month I'd be back on home ground in Salem. Instead of "how are you?" inquiries that referenced my bad relationship, pills, and therapists, I'd have an adventure to reveal. Instead of how I was, I was asked "How was your trip?" I was re-arranging my self-perception, and likewise the perception of others about me. I had found that swallowing the figurative toad of self-discipline and accomplishing what had previously seemed impossible lead to transformation.

A year into my trip, I felt better physically and mentally. I needed my inhaler less and for days I dispensed with it entirely. I didn't need pills for anxiety, so I gradually discontinued those. Something I had to address, though, was the pain shooting from my back down my legs that increasingly made it difficult to walk. When I first consulted with the orthopedist, he recommended a series of cortisone shots but they didn't help.

Eventually he performed surgery that he assured me would resolve the problem. For a while it was marginally better, enough that I could manage, and the RV living helped. But I was having increasing pain in my back and legs and grew determined to hold the orthopedist accountable for the surgery until he got it right.

I arrived back in Salem early, saw the orthopedist again, and got scheduled for another surgery in May. I insisted that this be the last one regardless of how drastic it was. The surgeon reassured me it would be resolved, and after that spring surgery, I surely hoped that it was.

I spent weeks getting back on my feet, but I had constant encouragement from Cricket and Magic, who needed walks. My surroundings helped too— it was late spring and I was in Salem. The huge snow piles of winter melted away and summer came full on. The coywolf reappeared, skulking behind bushes or buildings whenever I went out with the dogs. I delved into paperwork, and was relieved that I had fewer lapses in being licensed and authenticated than the year before. It was going smoothly—until I lost Milo.

Several years before, when I went to look at some kittens, Milo stood out. The others were playful and cute, but Milo was in a desperate situation of his own invention. He'd go dashing off, eyes wide, to survive some phantom monster attack while the other kittens envisioned no such demon. Milo lived in his own hilarious mind. Tiny and all black, he was my choice.

Milo was infinitely entertaining—someone could initiate a game of chase, or he'd just make it up. Anything the least noteworthy got Milo's extraordinary reaction. On seeing his first snow when I was still living in my Salem house, Milo catapulted toward the ceiling and I had to extract him from where he was hanging atop a door. Milo made the ordinary or non-event into the spectacular. He was so much fun, such a character.

So when Milo went missing I was devastated. While traveling, I was always either in the RV with Cricket, Magic and Milo, or not gone for long. But with the luxury of settled summer parking, one evening I joined a social gathering at Margaret's, just a few steps away from where I parked in her driveway. And on that balmy summer night, I accidentally left an RV window open. It was unusual not to have Milo in the greeting committee when I returned, but then he spent long periods in the upper bunk and maybe he had settled in the storage baskets.

But by the next morning, I knew he'd gone out that window. I couldn't accept his absence and convinced myself he'd be under the RV, around the yard, or that I'd hear him mewing somewhere down the street. I tore the RV apart in hopes I'd missed where he was hiding and searched the neighborhood. But no Milo.

To those who don't have a special bond with their pets, I guess there is just no explaining. I not only missed Milo to my core, but felt guilty in my negligence about the window. I made posters and walked the neighborhood again and again calling for Milo. The thought of the coywolf eating him froze my heart. His loss affected me for months that summer, like a gloomy veil over my subconscious, covering everything with a film of sadness. I did nutty things such as plan driving routes to take me past pet stores. I thought if I replaced him I might feel better—but then decided there was no replacing such a special friend.

One day in August, Margaret met me excitedly at the door. "Milo has been spotted!" she cheered. A fluffy black cat was showing up routinely three blocks over and a concerned woman left out cans of cat food for him in the evening. When she discovered his rhinestone and pink collar hanging in her driveway bushes, she was convinced he was a lost pet and made inquiries until the word reached Margaret.

I don't know if I walked or flew over to her house. I didn't see Milo at first, but noticed a suspicious hole under her porch. I looked in and there was Milo, much the worse for wear. He was emaciated and his Angora fur was matted, dirty, and unkempt. He gave a weak mew when he recognized my voice, and with coaxing came close enough for me to grab him. With Milo locked in my arms, I rushed back to the RV. Cricket and Magic recognized him immediately and welcomed him with attentive licks. During the next several weeks, I was able to return him to good health and slowly removed the snarls from his fur. I got Milo back, but was marked by the trauma of his disappearance and I never left the window open again.

In midsummer, I had another surgery. The second back surgery in May didn't cure the pain as promised, and my limping caused a malformation to form in one of my feet. The orthopedic surgeon was indifferent, but I found a sympathetic podiatrist who performed foot surgery. He split the main bone down the center of my foot, did skeletal alignment, and bolted it all together with pins and screws to keep the bones in their proper place. It was painful walking, but at least that surgery was successful, and eventually the foot healed for the better.

In the midst of this eventful summer, I drove the RV to a festival called Sirius Rising. I had a couple of good reasons to make the mid-summer trip. It's a festival gathering of like-minded individuals who join in a caring community of professed pagans—or whatever. But especially, I got to visit my niece Maia, her husband Rob, and his daughter Emma, as well as artistic and free-spirited friends.

It had rained heavily the week before I arrived, and I was instructed to park my lumbering RV in a suspiciously soggy field. I was not the first to get stuck in the field that day. Others RVs were rescued, but I was still stuck up to my hubcaps the next morning. A tractor failed to get me out, but finally a tow truck gave several explosive yanks on the RV frame that freed it from the mud. A motor housing in the back bedroom broke, and that slide-out never worked again.

This was another reality check for my limited repair funds, and I settled for a ninety-nine cent metal pin to hold the bedroom slide in place while driving. From then on, I manually pushed the slide open and closed as necessary, refitting or removing the metal pin each time.

I could sense the change over the years of my travel. I had been to Sirius Rising before as a newcomer, but now the event was a familiar reunion with Maia and her family. I am especially close to them and looked forward to the event all year. We camped in the woods, wandered among the vendors down a strip of dirt road called "the town," and decorated our tents and the woods with candles, solar fairy lights, and fanciful trinkets.

Nightly rituals celebrated air, water, fire, earth or spirit, and then a procession marched to a large bonfire prepared new each day. The drumming—and it was outstanding drumming including professionals—commenced and rumbled through the night. Everyone at Sirius dressed in festival style. We enjoyed unstructured time, and the atmosphere inspired a friendly and open spirit. I slipped naturally into the celebration of community, friends, and free living.

Years before the RV, I went on a kayaking trip to Nova Scotia. The expedition required a straight week of paddling around the tip of Cape Breton with a hundred miles of wilderness shore on one side, and the Gulf of St. Lawrence on the other. I had only what could be stuffed into my seventeen-foot boat, and it was my first experience living with just the bare essentials. I felt liberated.

There were thirteen of us on that trip, three guides and ten novice paddlers. We prowled the remote shores, shared dinners cooked on the beach, and star-gazed at the most marvelous sky I have ever seen at night. The Nova Scotia kayaking trip and Sirius Rising planted the seed of abandoning possessions, and allowing more time for friends, family, and fellow travelers in life.

I continued to make mental notes about where I might put down roots if or when I decided to find a permanent location. One of the first things you will hear from live-aboards on boats or RV full-timer wannabes is "no property taxes!" But that's incomplete and not quite true. One can let go of a tax-rent-mortgage home base, but it comes at the cost of always being on the move and disconnected from plumbing, heating fuel, and electrical power. The farther one is from utilities, the more you have to generate it yourself, exist with limited use, or learn to do without it. You will no longer take utilities for granted—your days will be taken up with hunting for services or coping in their absence.

Every stopping place wants something in exchange, like the rent for a boat slip, a campground spot, or the purchases I made at Walmart. Travel fuel becomes all-important and replaces the cost of property tax. If you travel less to save on fuel, you are still on the hook for the cost of space. Everything is a trade-off, and you have to determine what you can afford or tolerate.

State and national campgrounds have length-of-stay limits. Some allow parking for only a day, others for up to a month. Besides cost and availability, the camper should consider safety, location appeal, utilities, and fellow visitors. Some travelers seek solitude and time with nature, others bring civilization along with loud music and raucous parties.

I preferred integrating into interesting locations offering new experiences and immersion in local cultures. I liked house-sitting, but was spending large amounts of time securing each job. A house-sit had to be somewhere on my travel path, south in the winter or north in the spring. I had to get to know each host to see if the situation and my responsibilities were a fit. I could spend hours a day researching, messaging, and finalizing arrangements.

Not towing a car made navigating tight spots easier, but I didn't have the flexibility once I was settled. For house-sits, I depended on the host's spare car and learned to drive everything from a Lincoln that was so computerized it was scary—it automatically turned on wipers when it sensed rain —to a 1957 truck with the front seat frozen for a driver the size of Bigfoot. I learned and adapted well enough, but it was a constant effort. Making the car loan arrangement, worrying about damage to a host's vehicle, and repeating the process at each new house-sit began to drain me.

I considered motor home parks as a long-term possibility. But in May of my second year, the laws changed, and permanent residents had to be living in a verified "motor home (MH)," not a "recreational vehicle (RV)" like mine. A few phone calls confirmed that my vehicle, as comfortable as it was for me, would not pass the new housing restrictions. I considered trading for a park home, but balked at the price of something that would plunge in value the day after I paid for it.

Motor home park living can be relatively inexpensive, but it involves repairs, park rent, taxes, and utility payments similar to a traditional home. Repairs must be made when and how park owners dictate, often at their price. Lawns and exteriors must conform to their guidelines, and most do not allow dogs. New management might raise rent substantially. Theoretically, you can move the home, but at a prohibitive cost and with possibly nowhere to go. These contingencies reduce the resale value drastically, and many motor homes languish in trailer parks when people no longer want or can't afford them, can't sell them, and moving them is more effort and expense than they're worth.

I was now in my seventies, and so far in good enough health to continue my venture. But what if I wasn't? Health, my personal economy, or parking restrictions could catch up with me. I thought it best to make a soft landing while I still had choices. With that thought tucked in the back of my mind, I went to visit friends, Gary and Anne, in New Hampshire before finally heading back to Salem for the rest of the summer.

Salem as Home

Summer in the northeast is glorious. No one complains about the weather until they are looking into winter. Then the mantra becomes "Move south! Never shovel snow again!" But I discovered southern drawbacks, especially for a woman fond of the woods. The southern wilderness is a tangle of kudzu-covered swamps—there is no comparison with the open hardwood forests of the Northeast. Even on southern wilderness trails, I couldn't let the dogs run off leash for fear of poisonous snakes, alligators, fire ants, or a tangle of vines that could suck them into the equivalent of the Black Lagoon. My friends advised moving south, but increasingly I felt that settling north would be my best fit. Many didn't understand, but I was holding on to that thought.

For the moment, Salem and its unique culture was still home. Salem, the "Witch City," is an inclusive, tolerant, cosmopolitan, and cultured small city. Its citizens defy rules and norms when they consider them restrictive or unfair. Laws that forbid canines in restaurants are ignored, and instead dogs can enjoy lunch with their owners at sidewalk eateries—some offer special dinners prepared for dog companions. Salem residents worship their mayor, celebrate Halloween all year, and proudly embrace their colonial and maritime heritage. Street dress is anything you please, and it's not unusual to encounter pirates, colonial magistrates, or an unfortunate colonial maid being condemned as a witch since a play recounting the witch trials is enacted daily on the main street during the summer.

Salem residents were horrified when a woman who lived near Collins Cove went missing and foul play was suspected. To catch the killer, her body needed to be located, but the waters of the rugged ocean coastline refused to relinquish their secrets. After an exhaustive but fruitless search, the police consulted Laurie Cabot, Salem's head witch and psychic. As Laurie predicted, the body of Martha Brailsford was brought up in a fishing net near an offshore island frequented by lobstermen. Laurie also predicted that her killer was escaping to Canada, and with that information, he was apprehended at the border. With good policing and the help of Salem's occult, the murderer faced justice.

Spirits haunt Salem. While I found the Wiccan culture entertaining and respected its followers, I didn't consider myself a believer in such spirits. That is, until I heard the bells one night. I had gone to bed as usual, but sometime after midnight I awoke to the constant tolling of church bells that seemed only a few blocks away. It sounded as if they were tolling for the dead, and it went on for nearly half an hour. Now fully awake, I looked out windows, scanning the dark for signs of a commotion. But other than the bells, there wasn't a sound, a light, or a siren.

Then the bells went quiet, only to resume a few minutes later with wild rapid ringing that seemed a warning. The possible explanation of an after-midnight service gave way to my impression it must be an otherworldly signal of distress. Eventually I fell back asleep, but the next morning the vivid memory of the incessant sound of bells shrouded my thoughts. I called a few friends, but they hadn't heard the ringing. Around eight-thirty, my daughter called to say a family member had drowned herself during the night. An hour later, the news reported a Salem man had died in a fire. Both incidents happened at the time of the bells. I have never been able to shake that experience, and the line between rational events and Salem spirituality is forever blurred for me.

That summer in Salem, I embraced the culture of eccentricity and decided I'd paint the RV interior to match. My RV looked tired and dull inside, and diesel smudges stained the gray wall covering. But rather than pick a single color to live with, I brought home a paint palette of lime green, fuchsia pink, orange, Chinese red, soft blue, purple, and gold. Every square inch of interior surface in the RV claimed one of those colors. When I was ready to leave in the fall, I'd be taking the free spirit of Salem with me in those hues.

I began to mourn Salem in advance. I'd lived in my Salem home for fifteen years, just a few blocks away from Margaret's, but close enough to see the ocean. Now I parked at Margaret's in the summer and didn't miss Salem terribly in the winter. But I realized my situation was temporary—a permanent return to Salem would be difficult or impossible.

Salem is crowded with colonial houses packed so tightly in the old colonial working-class section that many are only inches from each other. Narrow streets trace the original footpaths and, bounded by the sea, there is nowhere for expansion. Only twenty-five miles from Boston by train, Salem's culture and location make it highly desirable and expensive. I could never buy my way back in.

Mid-summer passed, and somewhere farther north the first leaves were turning red and yellow. My things in Salem storage would stay put for another year, and I had more than I needed in my copious RV compartments. I carried the tools of my past projects such as leather-working, although I had no time for it. Pieces of leather, small tins of stains, and various cutting and carving instruments languished in the harder-to-reach places. I was giving up the idea that I'd have time and space for complicated craft projects.

I'd surely not be devoting endless days and obsessive energy on projects such as my Salem Haunted Dollhouse. I had seen a dusty, slightly broken Victorian dollhouse in an antique shop and loved its detail and lack of plastic. Charmed, I bought it and glued back shingles and delicate railings while my thoughts took shape. I painted, added wallpaper, and found rugs for each room. Then in mid-restoration, I removed all the rugs and wallpaper and started over, this time with tiny dollhouse wiring for electric lamps. It had not been intended for wiring, but over painstaking hours, I persisted. It was the most tedious, delicate work I have ever done. But the idea had taken over in my mind, and each room was eventually wired, with the wiring hidden behind the wallpaper and rugs I put back. After a month of intense work and concentration, every room had dollhouse-sized Victorian lamps and lighting.

I created the dollhouse to deal with my changing role in my family. I was no longer central as a single mother of three children. Creating the dollhouse helped me deal with the departure of my children and losing what I believed was my identity as mother. Each room had a different story to tell—my life raising children in an ill-fated marriage, adjusting to their independence, and re-establishing closeness through my grandchildren. I went back in family history, reviewed my upbringing and the impact of my sister's death that went forever unresolved by my parents. By putting all my family relationships in the dollhouse, I could revisit them, good or bad, but with the ability to move and manage the characters, to finally put them in their place.

In the upstairs bedroom a gremlin grandmother read stories to entranced grandchildren as a wise old owl sat beside her. In the other bedroom, the spirit doll of my infant sister who died in infancy slept serenely in her crib while kittens and butterflies in pictures watched from the walls as her guardians. I called it the Alice in Wonderland room and an effigy of Alice, only an inch high, kept company with my baby sister.

Downstairs, adult figures hosted a cocktail party with a slightly sinister overtone. I did it as a 1970s recreation of Ang Lee's movie, *The Ice Storm*. Pictures of kittens adorned those walls as well, but I imagined they were shaking their heads as the adults indulged in dark revelry. A pair of red shoes that knew there was no place like home overlooked a table holding bottles of alcohol, cocktail glasses, and a pot of warming fondue.

The kitchen was *Hansel and Gretel*, complete with a stove showing an open-doored oven. This was the only room with no characters, just a plate of fish on the table and an antique ceiling light that threw shadows about the room. Either the figures had disappeared into the oven, or had thought better of entering that room at all. Each room had some dread to contemplate or depicted a safe haven.

Such projects required considerable time and dedicated space to complete, which my wanderings from Walmart to Walmart didn't allow. The road trip itself would have to serve as the act of creation, with my three-year metamorphosis as the result.

The sound of crickets filled August nights. Purple asters and the reds and yellows of Indian paintbrush spilled vibrant colors through fields of late summer grasses turning brown and gold. Flocks of birds taught aerobatics to fledglings preparing for their first journey south. Everything hastened to enjoy the waning days and ready for the approach of winter. I decided on another trip to New Hampshire to say goodbye to Gary and Anne.

Milo had been found and was back, safe and sound, and the dogs were ready to travel. A much anticipated village fair filled the town center the weekend we arrived. Crafters demonstrated in their pop-up tents, food abounded, and music resounded from the town hall. I mingled and commiserated with locals I had come to know, and it was a happy day until I got back to the RV.

I was worried about Milo. His habit was to stay in the upper bunk during the day, moving from sunspot to sunspot. He would always acknowledge my arrival, though, and for the last few days he hadn't. I checked the top bunk to see how he was doing, and upon touching him, my heart sank.

Milo had an open sore that had burst through his skin. I knew enough about animals and veterinary ailments to recognize that Milo was very ill. It was the weekend, and I stayed by his side all day on Sunday. On Monday, I took him to the vet office where I agreed with the cancer prognosis and how far advanced it was. I gave my permission to prevent suffering and whispered goodbye to Milo as he let go of life in my arms. I nodded to the veterinarian as I left through a back door with Milo wrapped in a favorite blanket. I could say nothing. Later, I buried him at the edge of a field on Gary and Anne's property. I still go with the dogs to visit him when I stop by and keep his rhinestone-studded name tag in my jewelry box. Nothing can replace him, and I'm forever grateful for his playful company during the years we shared.

While grieving Milo, I had one more thing to face before leaving Salem. I had already had two surgeries that year, one on my back in May and the foot surgery in July. My foot was healing, but my back pain persisted, and I still limped because the sciatic nerve was being crushed. As far as I could tell from the x-rays, I had a couple of deteriorating disks that the surgeon had propped up with marbles. They were spherical implants intended to fit between and separate the disks. I didn't see how this would help any more than propping up the Tower of Pisa with a pile of marbles would since they were round, braced nothing, and I suspected weren't staying in place.

I finally convinced him that repeat surgeries were not in my future, so it had best be done right this time. With this understanding, I had one more back operation in early September. Post-surgery, I was assured it was a success—marbles removed, two cadaver vertebrae substituted for my disintegrated ones, and a construction of rods and screws to hold it all together.

I was totally exhausted after the surgery, but convinced the hospital staff I was well enough to return home. Poor Cricket and Magic. I was barely able to slide out of bed. I hired a dog sitter to walk them twice a day, but they were suffering with the minimal activity and confinement. I credit the dogs with pushing to me to get on my feet again, or I might have just languished there in the RV in Margaret's driveway. I gave myself two weeks' recovery time, which was nowhere near adequate.

Now it was me, the dogs, and chilly nights as fall slipped in. I checked GPS functions, explored MapQuest, and planned a general route for the third trip south. I had five months to fill with Walmarts and house-sitting, friends and family visits.

I had gained confidence and experience, but also depleted my resources. The broken motor for the back bedroom slide-out, well, I had learned to live with that rather than come up with seven hundred dollars to replace it. Leaks in the water tank drained away the few gallons that could be stored—the water tank was a losing proposition.

Water is heavy and uneconomical to drag along at the expense of fuel. From the storage tank, water circulates to the grey water or sewage tank, and then it's carried until one locates the next dump site, which is hard to find, deviates from the route, and costs ten dollars to use when you get there.

A plumbing system in an RV only has benefits when parked at a campground or for short trips. I learned to do with minimal water on the road. I washed clothes and showered when I house-sat or visited. In between, I made do with gallons of water purchased at Walmart for $1.29 each. Meals consisted of microwavable "heat in bag" vegetables, fresh fruit, and sandwiches. I cooked meat for the dogs or bought roasted chicken we shared. Cleanup used the least amount of water I could manage and still get the job done.

RVs are sold on the premise that you can duplicate home living in a traveling vehicle. That doesn't happen unless the RV is driven to a place where one hooks up to utilities. I calculated that if I stopped at campgrounds averaging forty dollars a day, that would amount to $14,600 per year, a hefty price for the use of utilities and a spot the size of a living room rug. Granted, I could make it more economical with discounted longer stays or at less attractive places, but it was still beyond my zero dollars for parking budget.

But I was not feeling deprived. I felt good (after recovering from the surgeries), enjoyed my days, and delighted in my ability to cope with most situations. I was free of former worries and dependency. I was free of therapists and medication to make one comfortably numb. I was clearer, sharper. I had cast off psychological moorings, tossed stuff, and lived by my wits. My dogs, the computer, and an engine that started faithfully were essential, but not much else. I made fun, I didn't buy it. Reaching the next stop was an accomplishment every day. I was becoming my own Lewis and Clark, striking off into territory where I found my own way.

The Third Trip South

My first stop was with friends I had made
through house-sitting in Connecticut. It's where I
met two lovely people, Helene and Fred, and their
amazing cat, Kitty. Kitty has cerebellar
hypoplasia. She could manage a halting walk
when I first knew her, but she was limited to a
feeble chase of a toy and had to be lifted onto the
couch. She was the perfect lap cat, so Kitty and
her owners formed a remarkable bond.

When I first met Kitty and her people, it was for
house-sitting. But as with others I met along the
way, we became friends, and I'd stop by whenever
I was passing through. I had spent hours keeping
company with Kitty, working in Helene and Fred's
garden, and learning the particulars of life in that
area. I walked the local fields of strawberries and
the acres of future Christmas trees. I collected

seeds from the garden and fields for some future garden I might have. Seeds and new friends—I was enriched and carried memories from every mile of my travel.

RV mechanics or systems continued to wear out, get damaged, and fail. I learned to live with less—and less. The radio had never worked and was now permanently disconnected. There was no hot water the first year, and by the second year there was no water. It would have taken a small fortune to repair the leaky tank. I limited myself to a couple gallons of water per day and learned to make that suffice for drinking, meals, and clean up.

Heat was never a problem since I installed the new propane system, but oh my, could it get hot in the RV. I was particularly exposed in vast parking lots, and without hookup there was no air conditioning. The dogs and I sweltered on hot days, and the last trip south the temperature was over one hundred in September. Plastic melted and parking lot blacktop steamed. I prayed for a breeze at night that would clear the stifling air out of the RV and allow us to breathe and finally sleep.

But on better days, the afternoons in the parking lots and free time when I was house-sitting left uninterrupted hours for study. I could indulge in an endless conglomeration of documentaries about wars, disease and medicine, national histories, geography, various economic systems, social movements, and biographies—the why, how, who, and where of just about everything.

I took notes, processed, and questioned some of my beliefs while confirming others. I think Wikipedia is the greatest gift to mankind, especially since it's a neutral reference on any topic. YouTube has videos of questionable facts and thinking, but also has a plethora of in-depth and thoughtful commentaries on historical events and contemporary issues. I was able to watch a six-part series on the history of the Middle East and follow the lives of notable writers, leaders, and inventors. I immersed myself in the lives and fates of the eccentrics, such as the notable tightrope walker Philippe Petit, who danced on a wire strung between the Twin Towers, and Annie Taylor, who was the first person to go over Niagara Falls in a barrel.

As I indulged in this self-imposed study, much

of my former teaching now seemed superficial and incomplete. I discovered how one country can imperialistically control another through finance alone, and how the bubonic plague gave rise to the English middle class in the 14th century. I didn't learn about the Crimean War in my formal education, but indulged in that history online. I was particularly interested in why wars started and what influenced world events behind the scenes. I gained a better idea of what started World War I and perhaps why it's never really ended.

I could tour the world in any time frame I chose. I looked at conspiracy theories, false flags, the shakers and movers. I learned about the machinations of the Dulles brothers in Central America and how an insurrection in Iran became a blueprint for future invasions everywhere. I spent days buried in *ProPublica* or other investigative news reporting. I followed explorers to the far ends of the earth and vicariously ventured into other cultures. Along with other countries, I got a revealing impression of our own.

I researched the history of every place I visited. Since I was in the South, I read and studied much about the Civil War. I learned why so much of antebellum Savannah is intact and why so much of Charlestown was destroyed. I learned how the lag of military tactics behind the improved lethality of weapons explains the horrendous death tolls and how issues regarding the burial of confederate soldiers contributed to resentments that linger to this day.

Mapquest and other geographical mapping programs are amazing. They made my journey possible and enhanced my travel experience. I could go forward and backward in space and time as I got to know the people, the geography, and how each piece fits into the puzzle of history.

While my perspective expanded, my meals got simplified. A staple was heat-and-serve basics— no cooking water or cleanup necessary. Warmed-over pasta was a regular. Luxury was a couple of hamburgers on the propane stove—one for me, one for Cricket and Magic. Cleanup was a wipe of the pan, a touch of soap, and minimal water to wash and rinse.

To my amazement, ice cream survived in the freezer. I snacked on cheese, apples, or a handful of nuts which I shared with the dogs. In the morning it was always the same—oatmeal, raisins, and a dash of water for a few minutes in the microwave. For some insane reason, I brought along a dozen cookbooks. While they were interesting to read, I was wasn't cooking for guests or parties. I ate out on stops with friends, but for myself and the dogs it could be as simple as opening a can of tuna.

This year, I avoided the much-beaten path of I-95 and stayed closer to the coast where it was warmer than inland. My body adjusted to the fluctuation in temperature between night and day, between one day and another. If it was chilly in the morning, I didn't bother with a jacket or sweater because in an hour or so the chill would retreat. All I needed to do was wait.

I learned to be cold and to be wet, and it was manageable most of the time. If you can get into a dry sleeping bag at night, especially with two dogs, you can cope. I thought back to my kayaking trips where there was nowhere to dry your clothes —you just keep wearing them and eventually they'll dry off from your body heat. The most you can do in a kayak is hang a dripping T-shirt off a paddle, but that's it.

Expecting to dry clothes, especially those made of cotton, in an RV is like throwing them in the dryer but never turning it on. You are essentially in a large tin can with all your moisture, sweat, and at times stagnant airspace. Being wet was tolerable, but excessive heat was brutal. In a Walmart parking lot, you can swelter.

Occasional discomforts aside, I had freedom from interruptions. For three years, I didn't answer my phone—who would be calling, anyway? The kids would email if the spirit moved them. I hadn't watched television for years before getting behind the RV wheel, so I didn't miss it. Surprise visitors were never at the door. I had no appointments, no To Do list. I was spared Muzak from shopping centers, waiting rooms, airports and bus stations, or any other venue that won't allow one to pass unassailed by noisiness. The only social chatter I encountered was with someone in line at Redbox, older women or teenagers commenting about my colorful hair, or a Schipperke admirer who stopped to ask about the dogs.

These were short, pleasant exchanges with strangers, but nothing that diverted attention from my deeper musings. Cricket and Magic were constant companions but demanded nothing except the immediate and relevant—dog dinner, walks, and lots of patting. I attended to food shopping, RV maintenance, and the driving, but otherwise relished the luxury of time for thought.

Especially in the US, sociability is a measure of mental health, but my personal assessment of wellbeing is the ability to live with one's self. I considered myself a mess before my RV trip. I had worry and sleeplessness, some kind of buried angst. Visits to counselors resulted in a dartboard of diagnoses and whatever was the darling drug of the day. You've made the visit, so it's you that needs treatment, and once you have a diagnosis, it might as well be tattooed on your forehead for any other medical person to read and evaluate. The "cure" is to show adjustment and get along with friends, partners, kids and bosses. No waves of discontent, no rage, no revolt. The shoe must fit— no matter how uncomfortable it is.

If you leave it all behind, you discover whether it's circumstances or you. After years on the road I felt fine, confident and capable, with no chemicals or somber weekly sessions. I had traded the highly profitable business of misery for the anecdotal 'long sea voyage.'

I decided to write and published a small book about my experience when Milo went missing. Completing *Milo* was cathartic, and next I wrote a murder mystery in which Helene and Fred's Kitty is a feature character. Kitty deals valiantly with her condition of cerebellar hypoplasia, and in spite of her physical limitations she contributes to the solving of a murder mystery. I was delighted when children coping with a similar condition were interested in and connected to the story.

The third year I started my journey south in September, so it should be pleasant days with crisp nights, right? Instead, it reached one hundred degrees for days on end. As I had in the bitter cold days of winter, I took the dogs into the Walmart entryways. I lingered an hour contemplating Redbox choices, just to extend the time in air conditioning. By bedtime, I stretched out on my steamy mattress with Cricket and Magic, who I'm sure wondered what we did to deserve this. There were four days when it was particularly brutal, and the dogs and I were not feeling well. By the time I got to Kathy's place in Maryland, I was heat-sick.

I collapsed in her air-conditioned guest room for a day before I felt reasonably recovered.

It was one of the best parts of my three years—visiting and catching up with friends and family that I might not otherwise see for years. Nothing involved or highly planned, just a casual drop-in and then "see you again soon" on my way back.

I made another stop to visit with my brother and his kids in North Carolina. Then I headed for the coast and a college friend, Peggy. She had sold her house and was now living on a boat, and I wanted to catch up with my fellow nomad. I got to tour lovely Newburn (later it was much damaged by Hurricane Florence). I thought about my decision to buy an RV instead of a boat. In spite of the marina being more attractive than a Walmart parking lot, for economy and safety, I decided I had made the best choice for my circumstances.

I drifted into the deeper south and visited with Sally and her five dogs again. With Cricket and Magic added, it was funny and crazy throwing balls around the living room for seven lively dogs. We visited a beach, discussed the hazard of fire ants, and I watched as Sally started packing for a move to North Carolina. I was grateful for my time there and Sally's guided tour of the area. I wondered if it would be my last visit to Beaufort.

The first year I had traveled deep into Florida, but this time decided not to go that far. I wasn't looking for an RV solar panel installer and it would have been hundreds of miles more. So it was January, and I was thinking about where I had been and where I was going in this pilgrimage to find myself. If I needed to stay put eventually, where would that be?

Decisions

Before leaving Salem, I had all my licenses and paperwork in order—I never did a repeat of the first year when I traveled blissfully along, unregistered and uninsured. I had dutifully taken the RV in for inspection before I left, but it was no longer fresh off the RV sales lot. It had accrued thousands of miles of wear and tear, and the mechanics told me it needed new ball joints and new brakes. An RV seems simple until you realize it needs the repairs for both a vehicle and a house. I had been lucky with my diesel engine, but if it needed major repair—which someday it would—it would set me back farther than I could afford.

Then I got the email from Margaret. It was a horrendous winter up north with one massive snowfall after another, usually only a week apart. Cars were buried, there was nowhere left to pile snow, and people just hunkered down in the isolation of their houses. This went on for months. Margaret was originally from California, and the northeast was proving too much to endure that winter. She said she would be selling the house and moving back to her home state. My friend and summers in Salem were going away. I no longer had the luxury of time to make a decision about where I would settle. I had to decide where home was, and soon.

I thought about my semester-long challenge with 'the egg.' While taking a course in graphic design at the Museum of Fine Arts, I was fortunate to be in Joe's class. Joe was funny, student-centered, and had a wealth of design philosophy to impart. At the beginning of the semester, Joe assigned us the usual design projects, a new one each week. About week three, I hesitated as we reviewed each student's most recent submission. When it came to mine, I spoke up and said, "Okay, that's fine, but I'm getting nowhere. I've been completing each assignment as if work is getting done. But I'm never any better. It's just another demonstration of the same skill level. I don't see that I've improved—I've just repeated a process."

Joe thought for a minute, then gave me a new assignment. "Draw an egg. Just an egg. Have an egg, paper, a pencil, and a lamp to cast shadow. Draw the egg over and over and nothing else for the rest of the semester. Don't do assignments with the other students. Don't throw away any version of what you've done. Keep it all in a sketchbook with bound pages and don't rip any out." So for the rest of the semester, the other students continued with weekly assignments, but I just drew an egg. Each week I presented my newest egg drawing along with the other students' current assignments. It was amazing.

Every week, my egg drawing was more 'an egg.' This may be based on how the Chinese and Japanese teach art. They specialize in a particular object—a tree, a rock, or a mountain. They draw that one thing for years, a lifetime, until they know it so thoroughly that it's no longer an outline or a solid or a color. They can draw the essence of the thing. I was learning that same lesson. I wasn't drawing just an egg, it was The Egg. When I showed my progress through the many pages of my sketchbook, it was clear what Joe wanted me to learn. My last drawing of an egg was a remarkable improvement.

I thought of this lesson regarding my RV odyssey. Even Ulysses eventually came to an ending, his journey complete, troubles vanquished, lessons learned. Either I was endlessly wandering, or I was finding a way home through these years. I was beginning to wonder about where my RV adventure would end. It was a necessary trip to clear mind, body, and soul, but at some point my diesel engine would give out and either I'd be stuck where my engine quit, or I could make a decision before the inevitable.

One last time I evaluated friends' advice to move south "for the weather–No Snow!" True that, but the heat of the summers is monstrous. I loved the northern wilderness and felt the outdoors was more accessible there. At any rate, that was my impression after three years, so I thought more about seeking a permanent place to settle north.

Living without running water and my bedroom slide not working was getting old. The last straw was the generator. It had been restored once by cleaning out the mud wasp nest in the vent, but it was on the blink again. I had little solar power on cloudy days, and now I rarely got the generator to start for back-up. It required fiddling with a switch in the back of the outside cargo storage, and sometimes it recovered, sometimes not. More of my time was going into repair and maintenance or worrying about it.

I was behind in my bodily maintenance as well. I hadn't scheduled an annual check-up or seen a dentist for three years. I was off the records with no address, and I neglected filing certain papers. The federal government forgave me about taxes since I didn't owe them anything, but without a paper identity, I was slipping away from benefits as well. For a reliable contact method, I was down to my email address, and that was only when I could access Wi-Fi. Pretty soon, I'd be carving messages on trees or sending letters in bottles I dropped along the highway.

I had a few things left in storage in Salem. There was no furniture, just lamps, rugs, and stacks of books. Besides the few practical things, I had collected artifacts such as a dagger made of cassowary bone from Polynesia and a stone carving of a walrus from Hudson's Bay. I had stored my last box of fossils, but continuing to pay storage fees for all my treasures wasn't sensible. I faced dispensing with even more stuff than I already had.

I was just short of lovely Savannah. I'd have liked to visit again, but needed to concentrate on my next landing for the summer. I spent my social capital with old friends and new that could give me a reference or a suggestion about post-RV living possibilities. I started to send out ads for my services as a long-term house-sitter or property manager. I passed by the cotton fields, the dollar stores, the countless little churches. I lingered less, made my plans for the next day and revised advertisements to post on Craigslist—mostly for New York, Massachusetts, and New Hampshire.

I reviewed my path south and back several times. I'd learned the territory, but what had been an adventure was becoming routine. The RV was aging, more parts weren't working and needed repair, and it was getting harder to find a place to park. Cities and towns were less tolerant of RVs, perhaps because they didn't like the homeless connotation. A few Walmarts were putting up No RV Parking signs in response to noisy diesel engines. Overall, more RVs were on the road with full-timers living in them, so a few RV vacationers were becoming more of an unwelcome glut. It was time to settle on more permanent plans.

I headed for a final visit with Kathy and Al in Maryland. I took unfamiliar back roads to avoid DC and the craziness of Route I-95. I swung far to the west of Manassas, avoiding the Washington Beltway with my push into the Virginia countryside. I went through Leesburg while following the advice of the lady in the GPS. She suggested that I could get to Dickerson, Maryland, across what I assumed was a bridge spanning the Potomac River.

The road got smaller and smaller, but it still accommodated the bulk of my RV. Any minute now I'd be at the bridge. The road twisted, turned, and led me right to the bank of the Potomac. But there was no bridge. Nor was there any hope of backing up. I had twisted my way down a winding slope while cars waiting for White's Ferry lined up behind me.

I stepped out of the RV to get a better grasp of my predicament. Absolutely, I was not backing up —I'd be stuck in a mud bank for sure. I looked across the river and saw a ferry the size of a short driveway. It was just a platform that promised to float about ten cars to the other side of the river. I judged the freeboard to be around a foot. I was too panicked to even sweat.

While the drivers behind me assured me there was no going back, I waited for the Lilliputian ferry to touch shore. A cheerful young man bounded off the deck and came over to talk to me —as I was surely a person that needed talking to. He assured me that he'd ferried a vehicle the size of my RV before, and that the odds of making it without sliding into the Potomac were good.

All I had to lose were my life, my dogs, and almost every earthly item I owned. The ferry docked, and with the young man's encouragement, I drove the RV onto the deck. We all had to stay in the vehicles, as it was a small ferry and a short ride. I unbuckled my seatbelt in case we sank, and gave a pat to the dogs. Since I was too paralyzed with fear to do anything else, I lifted my camera and took a few pictures out the window.

The chipper young man came over to my window to whisper advice that challenged my confidence in surviving this watery trip. He mentioned a sharp incline on the other side, so to avoid being stuck between the ferry and the riverbank, at the landing I should step on the gas even if my RV hit the dirt. "Don't get hung up," he warned, "just step on the gas—gun it and keep going. No matter what." I had no thought process left. I just absorbed his suggestion, sure that if I failed, it would be the last thing I would ever do.

A few minutes ticked by, and the ferry docked on the Maryland side. As the young man waved me off the deck, I increased the pressure on the gas pedal. I felt the tires tug and slip on the earth of the riverbank, and then the RV back end started digging into the ground. I pushed the pedal to the floor, and the engine groaned. The RV pulled, then jumped ahead as I started down the road into Maryland with a sizable chunk of Potomac riverbank hanging off the back.

Another visit with best friends in Maryland. Fresh sheets, a shower, clean laundry and a few more pleasant evenings would hold me until Massachusetts. We had cocktail hour at the end of the day and caught up on what's new and the kids. We talked of college days, people we knew, and those who have gone. I was glad to see my friends again, but this time it was bittersweet. I mentioned my plans to settle somewhere in the Northeast, either in the RV or... well, somewhere.

I was making contacts from the Craigslist ads. I listed my skills, focusing on property management and my computer savvy. I mentioned my hopes of a place to park the RV in exchange for services. I kept my eye out for people with a similar outlook on life, perhaps free spirits who loved the outdoors and got along well with all others. I was willing to trade casual living for minimal cost on my part and was happy to work for it. I was straddling my existence, one foot on the pedal, wandering from Walmart to Walmart down I-95, the other seeking a place that had little but woods and Wi-Fi.

While I was placing ads and writing back to those who responded, I rounded the elevated roads of Pennsylvania. Ghosts of the Civil War, so palpably alive and relevant in my travels south, were left behind in revered battlefields surrounded by split-rail fences and the vestige of trenches. Imagined battle cries fell silent as I entered the hum of contemporary enterprise.

There were two places in Connecticut that I

always enjoyed. One was Danbury, where they were always approachable, loved my purple hair, and adored the dogs. I had come to know and befriend people such as Lou. I'm still grateful for his help in giving me a place when I came through —our shopping for a thumb drive, his imparting the particulars of movie downloading, and cleaning out poor Cricket's eyes when she encountered a skunk in his yard.

I avoided Hartford one more time, but stopped to see Helene and Fred in Broad Brook near the Windsors. We shared another evening of politics, writing, gardens, and the love of miniatures, especially dollhouses. As always, I was enriched by the people I met.

Another night and I was close to home, but things weren't working. I was at Lowe's because it often had the strongest Wi-Fi. I also chose it because unlike the twenty-four hour Walmarts, it had a closing hour, so no one would know what I was up to in the darkness. I was running short of power and needed to at least charge my phone. I spent that night—long after closing—finding outside outlets and charging my phone. Like the beginning of my travels, I was getting less sleep and more stress as a result of power difficulties.

Massachusetts still felt like home, but it didn't feel as welcoming. There was no friend Margaret, no off-street driveway parking. I felt exposed and slightly persecuted. I moved the RV a couple of times a day. Instead of spending an afternoon at Walmart before settling for the night, I might be at the seaside park during the day but then move on as parking spaces emptied and I lost the cover of the day visitors. I'd join after-work traffic, then follow late night shoppers into the nearest Walmart parking lot. It had to be a twenty-four-hour superstore so I could blend in and look as if I had good reason to be there. After a few nights I'd make sure to do some Walmart shopping, and leave their bag near the door as proof of purchase in case some parking lot attendant or night duty policeman knocked on the RV door.

Landing

I was no longer immersed in the daily routine. Instead, I became preoccupied with where I could find refuge, a place where I could comfortably settle. I had to get to where living in my RV would be acceptable, and I could still have some of the free lifestyle I'd been accustomed to living.

I had three responses from my Craigslist ads. One was for a manager of three rental properties, the others were for organic farm help. The organic farms had places to park the RV for nothing and, theoretically, I would be sure of a healthy lifestyle and food. But there were practical problems. I would have no hookup for water, power, or Wi-Fi. Board consisted of soup or stew made by whoever was up for it, whenever they were up for it. But mostly, it was the Wi-Fi problem. I would be more restricted than in my Walmart parking lots in exchange for a full day's hard labor.

They were nice, friendly people, but I turned down the organic farm jobs and instead became a rental property manager in central New Hampshire. It was a lot of work with laundry, bed-making, securing reservations and troubleshooting the system failures, but I was good at it. I had a place to park and decent Wi-Fi. I was in the mountains, there were acres of blueberries, and the dogs had open fields where they could run.

My situation worked during the warm summer months. I got to know the state, its rules and requirements. But shortening days foreshadowed winter. Snow would make it harder or impossible to get out for propane. The solar panels would be useless when cloaked with snow, and it would be a challenge to get solar energy with low sun angles and short days. In my travels, there had been nearby motels, and the trips through Walmart aisles with the dogs in a shopping cart, but here there was just the endless woods—such a lovely escape in summer, but a challenge in winter months.

By August my back was up against the wall of oncoming winter. Harvest beckoned, fresh ads promoted school supplies, and flocks of birds practiced their long distance flying skills. I went back to visit Gary and Anne in Canterbury. Gary checked the RV to see how she was holding up and noticed a suspicious wire showing from behind a back tire. Closer inspection showed an infinite length of thick wire wrapped around the axle. It had likely been there some time, picked up as I went over road construction, catching hold of the axle, and then winding around it each turn of the wheel over the miles. Gary called it my "wire wheels" look. It took over an hour and two pairs of pliers for us to remove most of it, and some may still be clinging to that axle.

Anne and I took a long walk through the woods with Cricket and Magic. The dogs loved Anne because they associated her with a walk every time we visited. That, and Gary had two friends for them, Jack and Susie, Pomeranians that matched their size and lively nature. Later over tea, Gary mentioned that he knew of an inexpensive apartment for rent. I stopped over to see if there was potential, and found it had friendly landlords, they allowed dogs, and there was Wi-Fi.

This was the sensible, if difficult, thing to do. I would have shelter from the elements that had been such a challenge. I'd have relief from worrying about RV failures, especially if my diesel engine should finally falter. I'd worry less about freezing to death, and I'd have running water—even hot running water. I could get up in the morning and take a shower. I could just open the door and let the dogs out. It had what I decided was necessary.

But I'd be giving up visits with far-away friends, exploring new places, and the security of being in my place, my house, my RV. I had to face selling it before the Northeast winter depleted more of its aging value. To sell it with my cheerful interior paint job and the reluctance in my heart was a challenge, but I did it. A reseller in Florida answered my ad and offered me a much-reduced price in exchange for buying it unseen. My better sense realized this was the thing to do.

I steeled myself for the day the driver came to pick it up. It looked different without my funky, cherished possessions. The orchids in the window, the colorful baskets that organized my things, the random treasures I'd gathered along the way left empty spaces where they had been. The Tibetan flags hanging across the ceiling, the sweetgrass basket from the Gullah country, and the old sleeping bag that had insulated the bedroom window were gone. I left the spice shelf that Margaret had given me, but parting with the solar panels and Magnum inverter was particularly wrenching. The buyer wasn't interested in the solar set-up, and I suspected my investment in the system would be trashed. I ached about that one.

The driver with the check and the papers to sign would be here the next day. I took the RV out for a final run and goodbye. As I pulled her back into the apartment yard, I thought about my time living in her. I had lost the struggle to keep the RV in top repair, and her wounds—such as the leaking water tank and the troubled generator—were evident. But I had succeeded in managing my traveling home for three years and in the process had mended much in myself.

I had turned off the noise, turned within. I had been on the road or in a parking lot for most of three years. I entered Walmart for food and respite from the cold or heat, but that was it. I hadn't left the RV for more than a day, hadn't attended a concert or gone to a movie, mostly because of my meager budget and my determination to avoid places that wouldn't allow Cricket and Magic. I found a way to keep the dogs close, minimized distractions, and explored the world through backroad travel and roaming the Internet.

I had ditched pills, lowered my blood pressure, and lost ten extra pounds in spite of consuming much chocolate and ice cream. I had purchased next to nothing. Although I had visited many places, I mostly collected memories. I had left stuff and my own personal baggage behind.

I pulled into the driveway of the apartment where I would be planted, at least for a while. There was no more noise of traffic, no idling engines in the night, no rattling of something loose in the cabin. No sound of midnight rain on the metal roof. There was sunlight, bird sounds, the dogs barking as they raced out the RV door for the last time. I turned the key, the engine went quiet, and I was still.

The End

Made in the USA
Middletown, DE
13 May 2023